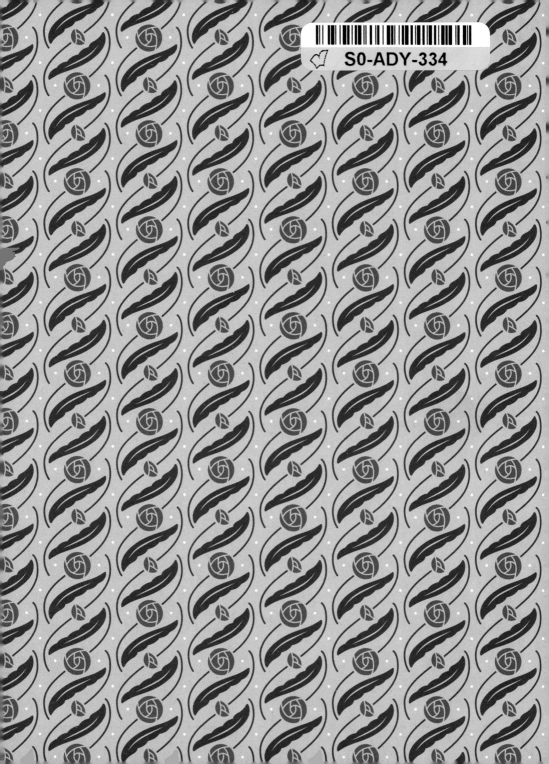

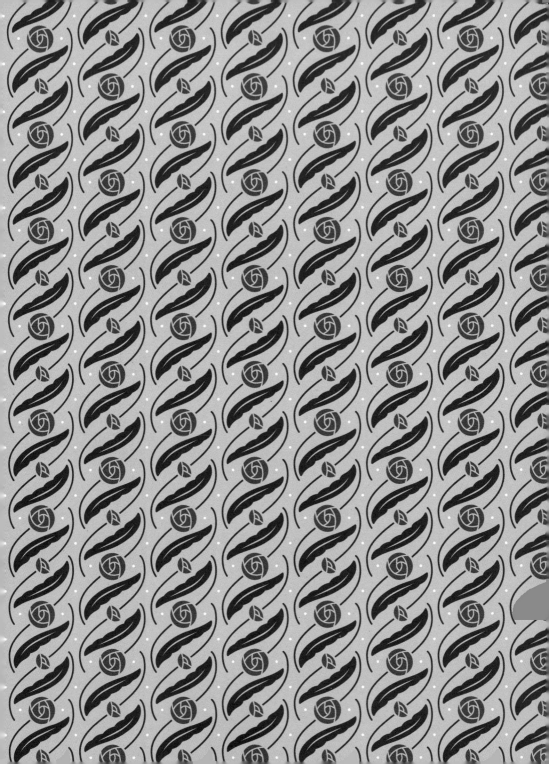

AESOP'S

FABLES

with Illustrations by
Walter Crane
Ernest Griset
and Arthur Rackham

BARNES & NOBLE
NEW YORK

This 2017 edition printed for Barnes & Noble by
Sterling Publishing Co., Inc.

ISBN 978-1-4351-6382-9

Barnes & Noble, Inc.
122 Fifth Avenue
New York, NY 10011

Manufactured in China

9 10

www.sterlingpublishing.com

Cover and endpaper art by Kelly Thorn

Contents

The Fables

1

THE TORTOISE AND THE HARE

THE HARE ONE DAY LAUGHED AT THE TORTOISE FOR HIS SHORT feet, slowness, and awkwardness. "Though you may be swift as the wind," replied the Tortoise good-naturedly, "I can beat you in a race." The Hare looked on the challenge as a great joke, but consented to a trial of speed, and the Fox was selected to act as umpire, and hold the stakes. The rivals started, and the Hare, of course, soon left the Tortoise far behind. Having reached midway to the goal, he began to play about, nibble the young herbage, and amuse herself in many ways. The day being warm, she even thought she would take a little nap in a shady spot, for she thought that if the Tortoise should pass her while she slept, she could easily overtake him again before he reached the end. The Tortoise meanwhile plodded on, unwavering and unresting, straight towards the goal. The Hare, having overslept herself, started up from her nap, and was surprised to find that the Tortoise was nowhere in sight. Off she went at full speed, but on reaching the winning-post, found that the Tortoise was already there, waiting for her arrival.

Slow and steady wins the race.

THE FOX AND THE STORK

A Fox one day invited a Stork to dine with him and, wishing to be amused at his expense, put the soup which he had for dinner in a large flat dish, so that, while he himself could lap it up quite easily, the Stork could only dip in the tips of his long bill. Some time after, the Stork, bearing his treatment in mind, invited the Fox to take dinner with him. He, in his turn, put some minced meat in a long and narrow-necked vessel, into which he could easily put his bill, while Master Fox was forced to be content with licking what ran down the sides of the vessel. The Fox then remembered his old trick, and could not but admit that the Stork had well paid him out.

A joke is often returned with interest.

THE PEACOCK'S COMPLAINT

THE PEACOCK COMPLAINED TO JUNO THAT WHILE EVERY ONE laughed at his voice, an insignificant creature like the Nightingale had a note that delighted all listeners. Juno, angry at the unreasonableness of her favorite bird, scolded him in the following terms: "Envious bird that you are, I am sure you have no cause to complain. On your neck shine all the colors of the rainbow, and your extended tail gleams like a mass of gems. No living being has every good thing to its own share. The Falcon is endowed with swiftness; the Eagle, strength; the Parrot, speech; the Raven, the gift of augury; and the Nightingale, a melodious note; while you have both size and beauty. Cease then to complain, or the gifts you have shall be taken away."

Contentment should be the source of every joy.

THE TWO CRABS

"My dear," called out an old Crab to her daughter one day, "why do you sidle along in that awkward manner? Why don't you go forward like other people?" "Well, mother," answered the young Crab, "it seems to me that I go exactly like you do. Go first and show me how, and I will gladly follow."

Example is better than precept.

THE FOX
WITHOUT
A TAIL

A Fox was once caught in a trap by his tail, and in order to get away was forced to leave it behind. Knowing that without a tail he would be a laughingstock for all his fellows, he resolved to try to induce them to part with theirs. So at the next assembly of Foxes he made a speech on the unprofitableness of tails in general, and the inconvenience of a Fox's tail in particular, adding that he had never felt so easy as since he had given up his own. When he had sat down, a sly old fellow rose, and waving his long brush with a graceful air, said, with a sneer, that if, like the last speaker, he had lost his tail, nothing further would have been needed to convince him; but till such an accident should happen, he should certainly vote in favor of tails.

Guard against those who would wish you to be reduced to their own level.

CAESAR AND THE SLAVE

DURING A VISIT THAT TIBERIUS CAESAR PAID TO ONE OF HIS country residences he observed that, whenever he walked in the grounds, a certain Slave was always a little way ahead of him, busily watering the paths. Turn which way he would, go where he might, there was the fellow still fussing about with his watering-pot. He felt sure that he was making himself thus needlessly officious in the hope of thereby gaining his liberty. In making a Slave free, a part of the ceremony consisted in giving him a gentle stroke on one side of the face. Hence, when the man came running up in eager expectation, at the call of the Emperor, the latter said to him, "I have for a long time observed you meddling where you had nothing to do, and while you might have been better employed elsewhere. You are mistaken if you think I can afford a box on the ear at so low a price as you bid for it."

Being busy does not always mean being useful.

THE WOODCOCK AND THE MALLARD

A WOODCOCK AND A MALLARD WERE FEEDING TOGETHER IN some marshy ground at the tail of a mill-pond. "Lord," said the squeamish Woodcock, "in what a voracious and beastly manner do you devour all that comes before you! Neither snail, frog, toad, nor any kind of filth, can escape the fury of your enormous appetite. All alike goes down, without measure and without distinction. What an odious vice is gluttony!" "Good-lack!" replied the Mallard, "pray how came you to be my accuser? And whence has your excessive delicacy a right to censure my plain eating? Is it a crime to fill one's belly? Or is it not indeed a virtue rather, to be pleased with the food which nature offers us? Surely I would sooner be charged with gluttony, than with that finical and sickly appetite on which you are pleased to ground your superiority of taste. What a silly vice is daintiness!" Thus endeavoring to palliate their respective passions, our epicures parted with a mutual contempt. The Mallard hastening to devour some garbage, which was in reality a bait, immediately gorged a hook through mere greediness and oversight; while the Woodcock, flying through a glade, in order to seek his favorite juices, was entangled in a net, spread across it for that purpose; falling each of them thus a sacrifice to their different, but equal, foibles.

A voracious appetite, and a fondness for dainties, equally distract our attention from more material concerns.

THE EAGLE AND THE CROW

A CROW WATCHED AN EAGLE SWOOP WITH A MAJESTIC AIR FROM a cliff upon a flock of Sheep, and carry away a Lamb in his talons. The whole thing looked so graceful and so easy that the Crow at once proceeded to imitate it, and pouncing upon the back of the largest and fattest Ram he could see, he tried to make off with it. He found that he could not move the Ram; and his claws got so entangled in the animal's fleece, that he could not get away himself. He therefore became an easy prey to the Shepherd, who, coming up at the time, caught him, cut his wings, and gave him to his children for a plaything. They came crowding about their father and asked him what strange bird that was. "Why," said he, "he'll tell you himself that he's an Eagle. But you take my word for it— I know him to be a Crow."

'Tis folly to attempt what you are unable to perform.

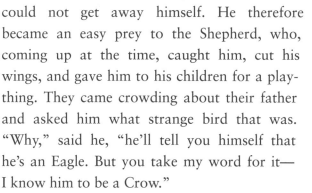

THE OWL AND THE NIGHTINGALE

A FORMAL SOLEMN OWL HAD FOR MANY YEARS MADE HIS habitation in a grove amongst the ruins of an old monastery, and had pored so often over some moldy manuscripts, the stupid relics of a monkish library, that he grew infected with the pride and pedantry of the place. Mistaking gravity for wisdom, he would sit whole days with his eyes half shut, fancying himself profoundly learned. It happened as he sat one evening, half buried in meditation and half in sleep, that a Nightingale, unluckily perching near him, began her melodious lays. He started from his reverie, and with a horrid screech interrupted her song. "Begone," cried he, "thou impertinent minstrel, nor distract with noisy dissonance my sublime contemplations; and know, vain songster, that harmony consists in truth alone, which is gained by laborious study; and not in languishing notes, fit only to soothe the ear of a lovesick maid." "Conceited pedant," returned the Nightingale, "whose wisdom lies only in the feathers that muffle up thy unmeaning face; music is a natural and rational entertainment, and though not adapted to the ears of an Owl, has ever been relished and admired by the best formed minds."

It is natural for a pedant to despise those arts that polish our manners, and that would extirpate pedantry.

THE MAN AND
THE LION

A MAN AND A LION ONCE ARGUED TOGETHER AS TO WHICH belonged to the nobler race. The Man called the attention of the Lion to a monument on which was sculptured a Man striding over a fallen Lion. "That proves nothing at all," said the Lion; "if a Lion had been the carver, he would have made the Lion striding over the Man."

Men are but sorry witnesses in their own cause.

THE FOX AND THE WOODCUTTER

A Fox, having been hunted hard and run a long chase, saw a Woodcutter at work, and begged him to help him to some hiding-place. The Man said he might go into his cottage, which was close by. He was no sooner in, than the Huntsmen came up. "Have you seen a Fox pass this way?" said they. The Woodcutter said, "No," but pointed at the same time towards the place where the Fox lay. The Huntsmen did not take the hint, however, and made off again at full speed. The Fox, who had seen all that took place through a chink in the wall, thereupon came out, and was walking away without a word. "Why, how now?" said the Man; "haven't you the manners to thank your host before you go?" "Yes, yes," said the Fox; "if your deeds had been as honest as your words, I would have given you thanks."

Sincerity is shown by the heart.

THE BOYS AND THE FROGS

Some Boys, playing near a pond, saw a number of Frogs in the water, and began to pelt them with stones. They killed several of them, when one of the Frogs, lifting his head out of the water, cried out: "Pray stop, my boys: what is sport to you, is death to us."

There are two sides to every question.

THE STAG IN THE OX-STALL

A Stag, hard pressed by the Hounds, ran for shelter into an ox-stall, the door of which was open. One of the Oxen turned round, and asked him why he came to such a place as that where he would be sure to be taken. The Stag replied that he should do well enough if the Oxen would not tell of him; and, covering himself in a heap of straw, waited for the night. Several servants, and even the Overseer himself, came and looked round, but saw nothing of the Stag, who, as each went away, was ready to jump out of his skin for joy, and warmly thanked the Oxen for their silence. The Ox who had spoken first to him warned him not to be too sure of his escape, and said that, glad as they would all be for him to get away, there was a certain person still to come whose eyes were a deal sharper than the eyes of any one who had been there yet. This was the Master himself, who, having been dining with a neighbor, looked in on his way home to see that all was right. At a glance he saw the tips of the horns coming through the straw, whereupon he raised a hue and cry, called all his people together, and made a prize of the Stag.

The eye of the master does more than all his servants.

THE MAN AND HIS TWO WIVES

IN A COUNTRY WHERE MEN COULD HAVE MORE THAN ONE WIFE, a certain Man, whose head was fast becoming white, had two, one a little older than himself, and one much younger. The young Wife, being of a gay and lively turn, did not want people to think that she had an old man for a husband, and so used to pull out as many of his white hairs as she could. The old Wife, on the other hand, did not wish to seem older than her husband, and so used to pull out the black hairs. This went on, until between them both, they made the poor Man quite bald.

No man can belong to two parties at once.

THE LION AND THE FOX

A FOX ENTERED INTO PARTNERSHIP WITH A LION ON THE PRE-tense of becoming his servant. Each undertook his proper duty in accordance with his own nature and powers. The Fox discovered and pointed out the prey, the Lion sprang on it, and seized it. The Fox soon became jealous of the Lion carrying off the Lion's share, and said that he would no longer find out the prey, but would capture it on his own account. The next day he attempted to snatch a Lamb from the fold, but fell himself a prey to the Huntsmen and Hounds.

Do not trust too greatly to your prowess.

THE BROTHER AND SISTER

A CERTAIN MAN HAD TWO children, a boy and a girl. The lad was a handsome young fellow, but the girl was as plain as a girl can well be. The Sister, provoked beyond endurance by the way in which her Brother looked in the glass and made remarks to her disadvantage, went to her father and complained of it. The father drew his children to him very tenderly, and said, "My dears, I wish you both to look in the glass every day. You, my son, seeing your face is handsome, may take care not to spoil it by ill-temper and bad behavior; and you, my daughter, may be encouraged to make up for your want of beauty by the sweetness of your manners, and the grace of your conversation."

Handsome is as handsome does.

JUPITER'S LOTTERY

Jupiter, in order to please mankind, directed Mercury to give notice that he had established a lottery, in which there were no blanks; and that amongst a variety of other valuable chances, wisdom was the highest prize. It was Jupiter's command that in this lottery some of the gods should also become adventurers. The tickets being disposed of, and the wheels placed, Mercury was employed to preside at the drawing. It happened that the best prize fell to Minerva, upon which a general murmur ran through the assembly, and hints were thrown out that Jupiter had used some unfair practices to secure this desirable lot to his daughter. Jupiter, that he might at once punish and silence these impious clamors of the human race, presented them with folly in the place of wisdom; with which they went away perfectly well contented. From that time, the greatest fools have always looked upon themselves as the wisest men.

Folly, passing with men for wisdom, makes each contented with his own share of understanding.

THE OWL AND THE GRASSHOPPER

An Owl who was sitting in a hollow tree, dozing away a long summer's afternoon, was very much disturbed by a rogue of a Grasshopper who kept singing in the grass beneath. So far, indeed, from keeping quiet, or moving away at the request of the

Owl, the Grasshopper sang all the more, and called her an old blinker that only came out at nights when all honest people were gone to bed. The Owl waited in silence for a short time, and then artfully addressed the Grasshopper as follows: "Well, my dear, if one cannot be allowed to sleep, it is something to be kept awake by such a pleasant little pipe as yours, which makes most agreeable music, I must say. And now I think of it, my mistress Pallas gave me the other day a bottle of delicious nectar. If you will take the trouble to come up, you shall have a drop, and it will clear your voice nicely." The silly Grasshopper, beside himself with the flattery, came hopping up to the Owl. When he came within reach, the Owl caught him, killed him, and finished her nap in comfort.

Flattery works better than threats.

THE ASS AND THE FROGS

An Ass, carrying a load of wood, passed through a pond. As he was crossing through the water he lost his footing, and stumbled and fell, and not being able to rise on account of his load, he groaned heavily. Some Frogs frequenting the pool heard his lamentation, and said, "What would you do if you had to live here always as we do, when you make such a fuss about a mere fall into the water?"

Men often bear little grievances with
less courage than they do large misfortunes.

ERNEST GRISET

THE EAGLE, THE CAT,
AND THE SOW

AN EAGLE HAD BUILT HER NEST IN THE TOP BRANCHES OF AN old oak tree; a wild Cat dwelt in a hole about the middle; and in the hollow part at the bottom lived a Sow with a whole litter of pigs. They might have remained there long in contentment, but the Cat, bent upon mischief, climbed up one day to the Eagle, and said, "Neighbor, have you noticed what the old Sow who lives below is doing? I believe she is determined upon nothing less than to root up this tree, our abode, and when it falls she will devour our young ones." This put the Eagle in a great fright, and she did not dare to stir from home lest the tree might fall in her absence. Creeping down to visit the Sow, the wily Cat said, "Listen to me, my friend. Last night I overheard that old Bird who lives over our heads promise her young ones that the very next time you went out they should have one of your dear little porkers for supper." The Sow, greatly alarmed in her turn, dared not quit her hollow.

The mutual fear of the Eagle and the Sow became so great that they and their young ones were actually starved to death, and fell a prey to the designing old Cat and her kittens.

Too much belief is worse than too little.

THE SICK KITE

A KITE WHO HAD BEEN ILL FOR A LONG TIME BEGGED OF HIS mother to go to all the temples in the country, and see what prayers and promises could do for his recovery. The old Kite replied, "My son, unless you can think of an altar that neither of us has robbed, I fear that nothing can be done for you in that way."

Be in health what you wish to be when you are ill.

THE COLLIER AND THE FULLER

A FRIENDLY COLLIER MEETING ONE DAY WITH A FULLER, AN OLD acquaintance of his, kindly invited him to come and share his house. "A thousand thanks for your civility," replied the Fuller; "but I am rather afraid that as fast as I make anything clean, you will be smutting it again."

Good conduct is often corrupted by false knowledge.

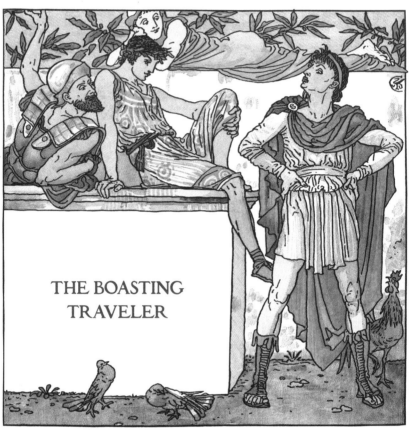

THE BOASTING TRAVELER

A MAN WAS ONE DAY ENTERTAINING A LOT OF FELLOWS WITH AN account of the wonders he had done when abroad on his travels. "I was once at Rhodes," said he, "and the people of Rhodes, you know, are famous for jumping. Well, I took a jump there that no other man could come within a yard of. That's a fact, and if we were there I could bring you ten men who would prove it." "What need is there to go to Rhodes for witnesses?" asked one of his hearers; "just imagine that you are there now, and show us your leap."

Seeing is believing.

THE ANT AND THE FLY

An Ant and a Fly one day disputed as to their respective merits. "Vile creeping insect!" said the Fly to the Ant, "can you for a moment compare yourself with me? I soar on the wing like a bird. I enter the palaces of kings, and alight on the heads of princes, nay, of emperors, and only quit them to adorn the yet more attractive brow of beauty. Besides, I visit the altars of the gods. Not a sacrifice is offered but is first tasted by me. Every feast, too, is open to me. I eat and drink of the best, instead of living for days on two or three grains of corn as you do." "All that's very fine," replied the Ant; "but listen to me. You boast of your feasting, but you know that your diet is not always so choice, and you are sometimes forced to eat what nothing should induce me to touch. As for alighting on the heads of kings and emperors, you know very well that whether you pitch on the head of an emperor, or of an ass (and it is as often on the one as the other), you are shaken off from both with impatience. And, then, the 'altars of the gods,' indeed! There and everywhere else you are looked upon as nothing but a nuisance. In the winter, too, while I feed at my ease on the fruit of my toil, I often see your friends dying with cold, hunger, and fatigue. I lose my time now in talking to you. Chattering will fill neither my bin nor my cupboard."

Bread earned by toil is sweet.

THE TWO POTS

A River having overflowed its banks, two Pots were carried along in the stream, one made of Earthenware and the other of Brass. "Well, brother, since we share the same fate, let us go along together," cried the Brazen Pot (who before that had been haughty enough) to the Earthen one. "No, no!" replied the latter in a great fright; "keep off, whatever you do, for if you knock against me, or I against you, it will be all over with me—to the bottom I shall go."

Equals make the best friends.

AESOP AT PLAY

An Athenian once found Aesop joining merrily in the sports of some children. He ridiculed him for his want of gravity, and Aesop good-temperedly took up a bow, unstrung it, and laid it at his feet. "There, friend," said he; "that bow, if kept always strained, would lose its spring, and probably snap. Let it go free sometimes, and it will be the fitter for use when it is wanted."

Wise play makes wise work.

THE WOLF AND
THE CRANE

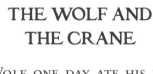

A WOLF ONE DAY ATE HIS FOOD so greedily that a bone stuck in his throat, giving him great pain. He ran howling up and down, and offered to reward handsomely any one who would pull it out. A Crane, moved by pity as well as by the prospect of the money, undertook the dangerous task. Having removed the bone, he asked for the promised reward. "Reward!" cried the Wolf; "pray, you greedy fellow, what reward can you possibly require? You have had your head in my mouth, and instead of biting it off, I have let you pull it out unharmed. Get away with you, and don't come again within reach of my paw."

Know those whom you would serve.

THE FLY IN ST. PAUL'S CUPOLA

AS A FLY WAS CRAWLING LEISURELY UP ONE OF THE COLUMNS OF St. Paul's Cupola, she often stopped, surveyed, examined, and at last broke forth into the following exclamation. "Strange! that anyone who pretended to be an artist should ever leave so superb a structure with so many roughnesses unpolished!" "Ah, my friend!" said a very learned architect, who hung in his web under one of the capitals, "you should never decide of things beyond the extent of your capacity. This lofty building was not erected for such diminutive animals as you or me; but for creatures who are at least ten thousand times as large; to their eyes, it is very possible, these columns may seem as smooth, as to you appear the wings of your favorite Mistress."

We should never estimate things beyond our reach by the narrow standard of our own capacities.

THE FARMER AND THE STORK

A FARMER SET A NET IN HIS FIELDS TO CATCH THE CRANES AND Geese which came to feed upon the newly springing corn. He took several, and with them a Stork, who pleaded hard for his life on the ground that he was neither a Goose nor a Crane, but a poor harmless Stork. "That may be very true," replied the Man; "but as I have taken you in bad company, you must expect to suffer the same punishment."

Evil company proves more than fair professions.

THE GOAT AND THE BOY

A Boy whose business it was to look after some Goats gathered them together as night began to fall to lead them home. One of the number refused to obey his call, and stood on a ledge of a rock, nibbling the herbage that grew there. The Boy lost all patience, and taking up a stone, threw it at the Goat with all his might. The stone struck one of the horns of the Goat, and broke it off at the middle. The Boy, terrified at what he had done and fearing his master's anger, threw himself upon his knees before the Goat, and begged her to say nothing to the Master about the mishap, as it was far from his intention to aim the stone so well. "Tush!" replied the Goat. "Let my tongue be ever so silent, my horn is sure to tell the tale."

Do not attempt to hide what cannot be hid.

THE DOG INVITED TO SUPPER

A CERTAIN RICH MAN INVITED A PERSON OF HIGH RANK TO SUP with him. Great preparations were made for the repast, and all the delicacies of the season provided. The Dog of the host, having long wished to entertain another Dog, a friend of his, thought this would be a capital time to ask him to come. As soon, therefore, as it fell dusk, the invited Dog came, and was shown by his friend into the kitchen. The sight of the food there filled him with astonishment, and he resolved that when the time came, he would eat enough to last him a week. He wagged his tail so hard, and licked his chops with so much vigor, that he attracted the notice of the head Cook, who, seeing a strange Dog about, caught him up by the tail, and after giving him a swing in the air, sent him flying through the open window into the street. He limped away, and was soon surrounded by a lot of Curs to whom he had boasted of his invitation. They asked him eagerly how he had fared. "Oh, rarely," answered he. "I was treated so warmly, that I hardly know how I got out of the house."

Beware how you accept favors!

THE FATAL COURTSHIP

A LION WHOM A MOUSE HAD FREED FROM A SNARE WAS SO grateful to the Mouse that he told him to name what he most desired, and he should have his wish. The Mouse, fired with ambition, said, "I desire the hand of your daughter in marriage." This the Lion good-naturedly gave him, and called the young Lioness to come that way. She did so; and rushed up so heedlessly that she did not see her small suitor, but placed her paw on him and crushed him to death.

Bad wishing makes bad getting.

THE TWO RABBITS

A RABBIT WHO WAS ABOUT TO HAVE A FAMILY ENTREATED another Rabbit to lend her her hutch until she was able to move about again, and assured her that she should then have it without fail. The other very readily consented, and, with a great deal of civility, resigned it to her immediately. When the time was up, she came and paid the first Rabbit a visit, and very modestly intimated that now she was up and well she hoped she might have her hutch again, for it was really inconvenient for her to be without it any longer; she must therefore be so free as to desire her to provide herself with other lodgings as soon as she could. The other replied that she truly was ashamed of having kept her so long out of her own house, but it was not upon her own account (for, indeed, she was well enough to go anywhere) so much as that of her young, who were yet so weak that she was afraid they would not be able to follow her; and if she would be so good as to let her stay a fortnight longer she should take it for the greatest obligation in the world. The second Rabbit was so good-natured and compassionate as to comply with this request, too, but at the end of the term, came and told her positively that she must turn out, for she could not possibly let her be there a day longer. "Must turn out!" says the other; "we will see about that, for I promise you, unless you can beat me and my whole litter of young, you are never likely to have anything more to do here."

Majorities promote tyranny.

THE TRAVELERS AND THE BEAR

TWO MEN ABOUT TO JOURNEY THROUGH A FOREST AGREED TO stand by each other in any dangers that might befall. They had not gone far before a savage Bear rushed out from a thicket and stood in their path. One of the Travelers, a light, nimble fellow, got up into a tree. The other, seeing that there was no chance to defend himself singlehanded, fell flat on his face and held his breath. The Bear came up and smelled at him, and taking him for dead, went off again into the wood. The Man in the tree came down and, rejoining his companion, asked him, with a sly smile, what was the wonderful secret which he had seen the Bear whisper into his ear. "Why," replied the other, "he told me to take care for the future and not to put any confidence in such cowardly rascals as you."

Trust not fine promises.

THE ENVIOUS GLOW-WORM

A HUMBLE GLOW-WORM LYING IN A GARDEN WAS MOVED WITH envy on seeing the effect of lights from a brilliant chandelier in a neighboring palace. When, after a short time, the light was seen no more, and the palace was left in total darkness, his wise companion said, "Now, you see, we have outlasted those many glaring lights, which, though brighter for a time, yet hasten the more quickly to nothing."

The meteors of fashion rise and fall.

THE SWALLOW AND THE SERPENT

A SWALLOW, RETURNING FROM ABROAD AND EVER FOND OF dwelling with men, built herself a nest in the wall of a Court of Justice, and there hatched seven young birds. A Serpent gliding past the nest from its hole in the wall ate up the young unfledged nestlings. The Swallow, finding her nest empty, lamented greatly, and exclaimed: "Woe to me a stranger! that in this place where all others' rights are protected, I alone should suffer wrong."

Do not place too great confidence in outward form.

THE FOX AND THE BOAR

A BOAR STOOD WHETTING HIS TUSKS AGAINST AN OLD TREE. THE Fox, who happened to come by at the same time, asked him why he made those martial preparations of whetting his teeth, since there was no enemy near that he could perceive? "That may be, Master Fox," said the Boar, "but we should scour up our arms while we have leisure, you know; for, in time of danger, we shall have something else to do."

The discreet man should have a reserve of everything that is necessary before the time comes for him to make use of them.

THE HARES AND THE FROGS

The Hares once took serious counsel among themselves whether death itself would not be better than their wretched lot. "What a sad state is ours," they said, "never to eat in comfort, always to sleep in fear, to be startled by a shadow, and to fly with beating heart at the rustling of the leaves. Better death by far"; and off they went accordingly to drown themselves in a neighboring lake. Some scores of Frogs who were enjoying the moonlight on the bank, scared at the approach of the Hares, jumped into the water. The splash awoke fresh fears in the breasts of the timid Hares, and they came to a full stop in their flight. One wise old fellow among them cried, "Hold, brothers! See, weak and fearful as we are, beings exist that are more weak and fearful still! Why then should we seek to die? Let us rather make the best of our lot, such as it is."

There are always some whose station is worse than your own.

THE ASS AND
THE SICK LION

IT WAS REPORTED THAT THE LION WAS SICK AND CONFINED TO his den, where he would be happy to see any of his subjects who might come to pay the homage that was due to him. Many accordingly went in, and fell easy prey to the old Lion, who devoured them at his leisure. But it was observed that the Ass very carefully kept away. The Lion noticed his absence, and sent one of his Jackals to express a hope that he would show he was not insensible to motives of respect and charity, by coming and paying his duty like the rest. The Ass told the Jackal to offer his sincerest reverence to his master, and to say that he had more than once been on the point of coming to see him. "But the truth of the matter," he observed dryly, "is that all the footprints I see go into the cave, but none come out again. So for the present my health demands that I stay away."

It is wise to see one's way out before one ventures in.

THE LIONESS AND THE FOX

The Fox once observed to the Lioness that Foxes were very much to be envied in the matter of fruitfulness. Scarcely a year passed that she, for instance, did not bring into the world a good litter of cubs, while some who had young only one at a time, and that not more than twice or thrice in their lives, looked down upon everybody else with contempt. This sneer was too pointed to be passed over in silence by the Lioness, who replied with a good deal of fire, "What you say is true. You have a great many children; but what are they? Foxes. I have only one, but remember that it is a Lion."

Prefer quality to quantity.

THE COCK AND THE JEWEL

A HUNGRY COCK, SCRATCHING FOR FOOD IN THE STRAW IN THE barnyard, happened to turn up a jewel. Feeling quite sure that it was something precious, but not knowing well what to do with it, he addressed it with an air of affected wisdom as follows: "You are a very fine thing, no doubt, but you are not at all to my taste. For my part, I would rather have one grain of good barley than all the jewels in the world."

A thing is of value only so far as it is of use.

THE LION, THE ASS, AND THE FOX

THE LION, THE ASS, AND THE FOX WENT HUNTING TOGETHER, and it was agreed that whatever was taken should be shared among them. They caught a large fat Stag, which the Lion ordered the Ass to divide. The Ass took a deal of pains to divide the Stag into three pieces, which should be as nearly equal as possible. The Lion, enraged with him for what he considered a want of proper respect to his quality, flew upon him and tore him to pieces. He then called on the Fox to divide. The Fox, nibbling off a small portion for himself, left the rest for the Lion's share. The Lion, highly pleased with this mark of respect, asked the Fox where he had learned such politeness and good-breeding. "To tell the truth, Sire," replied the Fox, "I was taught it by the Ass that lies dead there."

Better to learn by the misfortunes of others
than by your own.

THE LION IN LOVE

A LION ONCE FELL IN LOVE WITH THE FAIR DAUGHTER OF A FOR-ester, and demanded her of her father in marriage. The Man dared not refuse, though he would gladly have done so; but he told the suitor that his daughter was so young and delicate, he could consent only after the Lion's teeth were drawn and his claws cut off. The Lion was so enslaved by love that he agreed to this without a murmur, and it was accordingly done. The Forester then seized a club, laid him dead upon the spot, and so broke off the match.

Foolish love brings sorrow.

THE SHEEP-BITER

A CERTAIN SHEPHERD HAD A DOG IN WHOM HE PLACED SUCH great trust that he would often leave the flock to his sole care. As soon as his Master's back was turned, however, the Cur, although well fed and kindly treated, used to worry the Sheep, and would sometimes kill one and devour a portion. The Man at last found out how much his confidence had been abused, and resolved to hang the Dog without mercy. When the rope was put around his neck, the Dog pleaded hard for his life, and begged his Master rather to hang the Wolf, who had done ten times as much harm to the flock as he had. "That may be," replied the Man sternly; "but you are ten times the greater villain for all that. Nothing shall save you from the fate which your treachery deserves."

The most dangerous enemy is the one within.

THE SNAIL AND THE STATUE

A STATUE OF THE MEDICEAN VENUS WAS ERECTED IN A GROVE sacred to Beauty and the Fine Arts. Its modest attitude, its elegant proportions, assisted by the situation in which it was placed, attracted the regard of every delicate observer. A Snail, who had fixed himself beneath the molding of the pedestal, beheld with an evil eye the admiration it excited. Wherefore, watching his opportunity, he strove, by trailing his filthy slime over every limb and feature, to obliterate those beauties that he could not endure to hear so much applauded. An honest Linnet, however, who observed him at his dirty work, took the freedom to assure him that he would infallibly lose his labor: "For although," said he, "to an injudicious eye, thou mayst sully the perfections of this finished piece; yet a more accurate and close inspector will admire its beauty, through all the blemishes with which thou hast endeavored to disguise it."

It is the fate of envy to attack even those characters which are superior to its malice.

THE SERPENT AND THE MAN

THE CHILD OF A VILLAGER, WHILE AT PLAY IN A FIELD AT THE back of his Father's house, by chance trod upon a Snake, which turned round and bit him. The Child died of the bite, and the Father, pursuing the Snake, aimed a blow at him, and cut off a piece of his tail. The Snake gained his hole, and the next day the Man came and laid at the mouth of the hole some honey, meal, and salt, and made offers of peace, thinking to entice the Snake forth and kill him. "It won't do," hissed out the Snake. "As long as I miss my tail, and you your Child, there can be no good-will between us."

A false truce is worse than battle.

THE DOG AND HIS SHADOW

A DOG, BEARING IN HIS MOUTH A PIECE OF MEAT THAT HE HAD stolen, was crossing a smooth stream by means of a plank. Looking in, he saw what he took to be another dog carrying another piece of meat. Snapping greedily to get this as well, he let go the meat that he had, and lost it in the stream.

Catch at the shadow and you lose the substance.

THE FOX AND THE APE

UPON THE DECEASE OF THE LION, THE BEASTS OF THE FOREST assembled to choose another king. The Ape made so many grimaces, and played so many antic tricks, that he was elected by a large majority, and the crown was placed upon his head. The Fox, envious of this distinction, seeing soon after a trap baited with a piece of meat, approached the new king, and said with mock humility, "May it please your majesty, I have found on your domain a treasure to which, if you will deign to accompany me, I will conduct you." The Ape thereupon set off with the Fox, and on arriving at the spot, laid his paw upon the meat. Snap! went the trap, and caught him by the fingers. Mad with the shame and the pain, he called the Fox a thief and a traitor. The Fox laughed heartily and, going off, said over his shoulder, with a sneer, "You a king, and not understand a trap!"

Those who cannot manage their own affairs
are unfit to manage others'.

THE STAG AND THE FAWN

A FAWN ONCE SAID TO A STAG, "HOW IS IT THAT YOU, WHO ARE so much bigger, and stronger, and fleeter than a Dog, are in such a fright when you behold one? If you stood your ground, and used your horns, I should think the Hounds would fly from you." "I have said that to myself, little one, over and over again," replied the Stag, "and made up my mind to act upon it; but yet, no sooner do I hear the voice of a Dog than I am ready to jump out of my skin."

*No **arguments** will give courage to a coward.*

THE FALCONER AND THE PARTRIDGE

A PARTRIDGE, BEING TAKEN IN THE NET OF A FALCONER, BEGGED hard of the Man to be set free, and promised if he were let go to decoy other Partridges into the net. "No," replied the Falconer; "I did not mean to spare you; but, if I had, your words would now have condemned you. The scoundrel who, to save himself, offers to betray his friends, deserves worse than death."

Better a death with honor than a life with shame.

THE MISER

A MISER ONCE BURIED ALL HIS MONEY IN THE EARTH, AT THE foot of a tree, and went every day to feast upon the sight of his treasure. A thievish fellow, who had watched him at this occupation, came one night and carried off the gold. The next day the Miser, finding his treasure gone, tore his clothes and filled the air with his lamentations. A neighbor hearing his outcry and learning the cause said, "Pray do not grieve so; but go and get a stone, place it in the hole, and fancy it is your gold. It will be of quite as much service as the money was."

Wealth not used is of no value at all.

THE SHIPWRECKED MAN
AND THE SEA

A SHIPWRECKED MAN CAST UP ON THE BEACH FELL ASLEEP AFTER his struggle with the waves. When he woke up, he bitterly reproached the sea for its treachery in enticing men with its smooth and smiling surface, and then, when they were well embarked, turning in fury upon them and sending both ship and sailors to destruction. The sea arose in the form of a woman, and replied, "Lay not the blame on me, sailor, but on the winds. By nature I am as calm and safe as the land itself: but the winds fall upon me with their gusts and gales, and lash me to a fury that is not natural to me."

Place blame where it is due.

A MAN BITTEN BY A DOG

A MAN WHO HAD BEEN BITTEN BY A DOG WAS ADVISED BY AN old woman to cure the wound by rubbing a piece of bread in it, and giving it to the Dog that had bitten him. He did so, and Aesop, passing by at the time, asked him what he was about. The Man told him, and Aesop replied, "I am glad you do it privately, for if the rest of the Dogs of the town were to see you, we should be eaten up alive."

Season counsel with sense.

THE LION AND THE SLAVE

A RUNAWAY SLAVE ONCE MET UP WITH A LION WHO HAD TROD upon a thorn, and who came up towards him wagging his tail, and holding up his lame foot, as if he would say, "I am a suppliant, and seek your aid." The Slave boldly examined the wound, discovered the thorn, and placing the Lion's foot upon his lap, pulled it out and relieved the animal of his pain. The Lion joyfully returned to the forest. Some time after, the Slave was captured and was condemned to be cast to the Lion. The Lion proved to be the one he had befriended. On being released from his cage, he recognized the Slave as the man who had healed him, and, instead of attacking him, approached and placed his foot upon the man's lap. The King, as soon as he had heard the tale, ordered the Lion to be set free again in the forest, and the Slave to be pardoned and given his liberty.

One good deed deserves another.

THE MAN AND THE WEASEL

A MAN CAUGHT A WEASEL AND WAS ABOUT TO KILL IT. THE LITTLE animal prayed earnestly for his life. "You will not be so unkind," said he to the Man, "as to slay a poor creature who kills your Mice for you?" "For me!" answered the Man; "that's a good joke. For me, you say, as if you did not catch them more for your own pleasure than for my profit. And as to making away with my food, you know that you do as much harm as the Mice themselves. You must make some better excuse than that, before I shall feel inclined to spare you." Having said this, he strangled the Weasel without more ado.

A poor excuse is a dangerous thing.

THE VIPER AND THE FILE

A Viper entered a smith's shop and looked up and down for something to eat. He settled at last upon a File, and began to gnaw it greedily. "Bite away," said the File gruffly, "you'll get little from me. It is my business to take from all and give to none."

Before you attack, know thine enemy.

AESOP'S FABLES

THE HUNTER, THE FOX, AND THE TIGER

A CERTAIN HUNTER SAW, IN THE MIDDLE OF A FIELD, A FOX whose skin was so beautiful that he wished to take him alive. Having this in view, he found out his hole, and just before the entrance to it he dug a large and deep pit, covered it with slender twigs and straw, and placed a piece of horseflesh on the middle of the covering. When he had done this he went and hid himself in a corner out of sight, and the Fox, returning to his hole and smelling the flesh, ran up to see what dainty morsel it was. When he came to the pit he would fain have tasted the meat, but fearing some trick he refrained from doing so, and retreated into his hole. Presently, up came a hungry Tiger, who, being tempted by the smell and appearance of the horseflesh, sprang in haste to seize it, and tumbled into the pit. The Hunter, hearing the noise made by the Tiger in falling, ran up and jumped into the pit without looking into it, never doubting that it was the Fox that had fallen in. But there, to his surprise, he found the Tiger, which quickly tore him in pieces and devoured him.

Look before you leap.

THE ROBIN AND THE SPARROW

AS A ROBIN WAS SINGING ON A TREE BY THE SIDE OF A RURAL cottage, a Sparrow perched upon the thatch took occasion thus to reprimand him: "And dost thou," said he, "with thy dull autumnal note, presume to emulate the birds of spring? Can thy weak warblings pretend to vie with the sprightly accents of the Thrush and Blackbird, with the various melodies of the Lark or Nightingale, whom other birds far thy superiors, have long been content to admire in silence?" "Judge with candor at least," replied the Robin, "nor impute those efforts to ambition solely, which may sometimes flow from the love of art. I reverence, indeed, but by no means envy, the birds whose fame has stood the test of ages. Their songs have charmed both hill and dale, but their season is past, and their throats are silent. I feel not, however, the ambition to surpass or equal them; my efforts are of a much humbler nature, and I may surely hope for pardon, while I endeavor to cheer these forsaken valleys, by an attempt to imitate the strains I love."

Imitation may be pardonable where emulation would be presumptuous.

THE THRUSH AND THE FOWLER

A Thrush was feeding on a myrtle tree, and did not move from it, on account of the deliciousness of its berries. A Fowler observing her staying so long in one spot, having well bird-limed his reeds, caught her. The Thrush, being at the point of death, exclaimed, "O foolish creature that I am! For the sake of a little pleasant food I have deprived myself of my life."

Do not lose sight of the future in the present.

THE GOOSE THAT LAID
THE GOLDEN EGGS

A CERTAIN MAN HAD A GOOSE THAT LAID HIM A GOLDEN EGG every day. Being of a covetous turn, he thought if he killed his Goose he should come at once to the source of his treasure. So he killed her, and cut her open, when great was his dismay to find that her inside was in no way different from that of any other Goose.

Greediness overreaches itself.

THE ASS AND THE LITTLE DOG

THE ASS, OBSERVING HOW GREAT A FAVORITE A LITTLE DOG WAS with his Master—how much caressed, and fondled, and fed with choice bits at every meal, and for no other reason that he could see, but skipping and frisking about and wagging his tail—resolved to imitate him, and see whether the same behavior would not bring him similar favors. Accordingly, the Master was no sooner come home from walking, and seated in his easy-chair, than the Ass came into the room, and danced around him with many an awkward gambol. The Man could not help laughing aloud at the odd sight. The joke, however, became serious, when the Ass, rising on his hind-legs, laid his forefeet upon his Master's shoulders, and braying in his face in the most fascinating manner, would fain have jumped into his lap. The Man cried out for help, and one of his servants running in with a good stick, laid it unmercifully on the bones of the poor Ass, who was glad to get back to his stable.

A place for everyone, and everyone in his place.

THE BEE AND THE FLY

A Bee, observing a Fly frisking about her hive, asked him in a very angry tone what he did there. "Is it for such fellows as you," said she, "to intrude into the company of the queens of the air?" "You have great reason, truly," replied the Fly, "to be out of humor. I am sure they must be mad who would have any concern with so quarrelsome a nation." "And why so, may I ask?" returned the enraged Bee. "We have the best laws and are governed by the best policy in the world. We feed upon the most fragrant flowers, and all our business is to make honey; honey, which equals nectar, low, tasteless wretch, who lives upon nothing but vile things." "We live as we can," rejoined the Fly. "Poverty, I hope, is no crime; but passion is one, I am sure. The honey you make is sweet, I grant you, but your heart is all bitterness; for to be revenged on an enemy you will destroy your own life, and are so foolish in your rage as to do more mischief to yourselves than to your enemy. Take my word for it, one had better have fewer talents, and use them more wisely."

Well-governed communities should make
well-governed individuals.

THE WIND AND THE SUN

A DISPUTE ONCE AROSE BETWEEN THE NORTH
Wind and the Sun as to which was the stronger of the two. Seeing a Traveler on his way, they
agreed to see which could the sooner get his cloak off him.
The North Wind began, and sent a furious blast, which, at the
onset, nearly tore the cloak from its fastenings; but the Traveler, seizing the garment with a firm grip, held it round his
body so tightly that the North Wind spent his remaining force
in vain. The Sun, dispelling the clouds that had gathered, then

darted his genial beams on the Traveler's head. Growing faint with the heat, the Man flung off his coat, and ran for protection to the nearest shade.

Mildness governs more than anger.

THE TWO SPRINGS

Two Springs which issued from the same mountain began their course together; one of them took her way in a silent and gentle stream, while the other rushed along with a sounding and rapid current. "Sister," said the latter, "at the rate you move, you will probably be dried up before you advance much farther; whereas, for myself, I will venture a wager, that within two or three hundred furlongs I shall become navigable, and after distributing commerce and wealth wherever I flow, I shall majestically proceed to pay my tribute to the ocean: so farewell, dear sister, and patiently submit to your fate." Her sister made no reply, but calmly descending to the meadows below, increased her stream by numberless little rills, which she collected in her progress, till at length she was enabled to rise into a considerable river; while the proud stream, which had the vanity to depend solely upon her own sufficiency, continued a shallow brook, and was glad at last to be helped forward, by throwing herself into the arms of her despised sister.

There is more to be expected from sedate and silent, than from noisy, turbulent, and ostentatious beginnings.

THE FOX AND THE MOSQUITOES

A Fox was being tormented by a swarm of Mosquitoes. When another Fox offered to shoo them away, the first Fox declined. "They will only be replaced by a hungrier swarm," he said. "I had rather the full ones stay."

Better a lesser problem than a worse one.

THE GOATHERD AND THE GOATS

During a snowstorm in the depth of winter, a Goatherd drove his Goats for shelter to a large cavern in a rock. It happened that some wild Goats had already taken refuge there. The Man was so struck by the size and look of these Goats, and with their superior beauty to his own, that he gave to them all the food he could collect. The storm lasted many days, and the tame Goats, being entirely without food, died of starvation. As soon as the sun shone again, the strangers ran off, and made the best of their way to their native wilds. "Ungrateful beasts!" cried he, "is this the way you reward him who has served you?" "How do we know," replied the last of the departing flock, "that you will not forsake your new friends in time of need, even as you forsook your old ones?" So the Goatherd had to go goatless home, and was well laughed at by all for his folly.

Be true to your own.

INDUSTRY AND SLOTH

AN INDOLENT YOUNG MAN, BEING ASKED WHY HE LAY IN BED SO long, jocosely and carelessly answered: "Every morning of my life I hear long causes. I have two fine girls, named Industry and Sloth, close at my bedside, as soon as ever I awake, pressing their different suits. One entreats me to get up, the other persuades me to lie still; and then they alternately give me various reasons why I should rise, and why I should not. In the meantime, as it is the duty of an impartial judge to hear all that can be said on either side, before the pleadings are over, it is time to go to dinner."

The lazy have more excuses for their sloth
than the productive have for their industry.

THE MOON AND HER MOTHER

THE MOON ONCE BEGGED HER MOTHER TO MAKE HER A GOWN. "How can I," replied she; "there's no fitting your figure. At one time you're a New Moon, at another you're a Full Moon; and between whiles you're neither one nor the other."

There is no pleasing the fickle.

THE POWER OF FABLES

DEMADES, A FAMOUS GREEK ORATOR, WAS ONCE ADDRESSING AN assembly at Athens on a subject of great importance, and in vain tried to fix the attention of his hearers. They laughed among themselves, watched the sports of the children, and in twenty other ways showed their want of concern in the subject of the discourse. Demades, after a short pause, spoke as follows: "Ceres one day journeyed in company with a Swallow and an Eel." At this there was marked attention, and every ear strained now to catch the words of the orator. "The party came to a river," continued he. "The Eel swam across, and the Swallow flew over." He then resumed the subject of his harangue. A great cry, however, arose from the people. "And Ceres? And Ceres?" cried they. "What did Ceres do?" "Why, the goddess was, and indeed she is now," replied he, "mightily offended that people should have their ears open to any sort of foolery, and shut to words of truth and wisdom."

Learn to listen wisely.

THE ASS, THE LION, AND THE COCK

AN ASS AND A COCK, FEEDING IN THE SAME MEADOW, WERE ONE day surprised by a Lion. The Cock crowed loudly, and the Lion (who is said to have a great antipathy to the crowing of a Cock) at once turned tail and ran off again. The Ass, believing that it was from fear of him that the Lion fled, pursued him. As soon as they were out of hearing of the Cock, the Lion turned round upon the Ass and tore him in pieces.

False confidence leads one to danger.

THE OLD WOMAN AND THE DOCTOR

AN OLD WOMAN WHO HAD BAD EYES CALLED IN A CLEVER Doctor, who agreed for a certain sum to cure them. He was a very clever Doctor, but he was also a very great rogue; and when he called each day and bound up the Old Woman's eyes, he took advantage of her blindness to carry away with him some article of her furniture. This went on until he pronounced the Woman cured. Her room was then nearly bare. He claimed his reward, but the Old Lady protested that, so far from being cured, her sight was worse than ever. "We will soon see about that, my good Woman," said he; and she was shortly after summoned to appear in Court. "May it please your Honor," said she to the Judge, "before I called in this Doctor I could see a score of things in my room that now, when he says I am cured, I cannot see at all." This opened the eyes of the Court to the knavery of the Doctor, who was forced to give the Old Woman her property back again, and was not allowed to claim a penny of his fee.

Knavery overreaches itself.

THE HUNTER AND THE WOODMAN

A HUNTER WAS SEARCHING IN THE FOREST FOR THE TRACKS OF A Lion, and, catching sight presently of a Woodman engaged in felling a tree, he went up to him and asked him if he had noticed a Lion's footprints anywhere about, or if he knew where his den was. The Woodman answered, "If you will come with me, I will show you the Lion himself." The Hunter turned pale with fear, and his teeth chattered as he replied, "Oh, I'm not looking for the Lion, thanks, but only for his tracks."

What some seek in sport they would shun in earnest.

FORTUNE AND
THE BOY

A LITTLE BOY, QUITE TIRED OUT WITH PLAY, STRETCHED OUT, and fell sound asleep close to the edge of a deep well. Fortune came by and, gently waking him, said, "My dear Boy, believe me, I have saved your life. If you had fallen in, everybody would have laid the blame on me; but tell me truly, now, would the fault have been yours or mine?"

Lay the blame where it belongs.

THE APE AND THE DOLPHIN

A SHIP, WRECKED OFF THE COAST OF GREECE, HAD ON BOARD A large Ape, kept for the diversion of the sailors. The ship went down, and the Ape, with most of the crew, was left struggling in the water. Dolphins are said to have a great friendship for man; and one of these fishes, taking the Ape for a man, came under him, and, supporting him on his back, swam with him to the mouth of the harbor of Piraeus. "In what part of Greece do you live?" demanded the Dolphin. "I am an Athenian," said the Ape. "Oh, then, you know Piraeus, of course?" said the Dolphin. "Know Piraeus!" said the Ape, not wishing to appear ignorant to the Dolphin; "I should rather think I did. Why, my father and he are first cousins." Thereupon the Dolphin, finding that he was supporting an impostor, slipped from beneath his legs, and left him to his fate.

The liar should take care to be well informed.

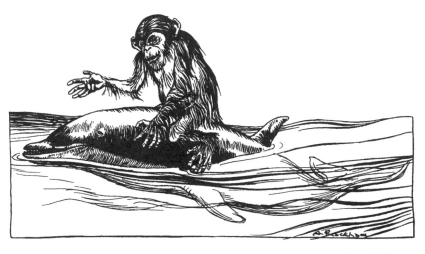

THE WOLF AND THE LAMB

A HUNGRY WOLF ONE DAY saw a Lamb drinking at a stream below him and wished to find some excuse for eating her. "What do you mean by muddying the water I am going to drink?" said he fiercely to the Lamb. "Pray forgive me," meekly answered the Lamb; "I should be sorry in any way to displease you, but as the stream runs from you towards me, you will see that I am not to blame." "That's all very well," said the Wolf; "but you know you spoke ill of me behind my back a year ago." "Nay, believe me," replied the Lamb, "I was not then born." "It must have been your brother, then," growled the Wolf. "It cannot have been, for I never had any," answered the Lamb. "I know it was one of your lot," rejoined the Wolf, "so make no more such idle excuses." He then seized the poor Lamb, carried her off to the woods, and ate her.

The wicked always finds an excuse for wrongdoing.

JUPITER AND THE BEE

A BEE MADE JUPITER A PRESENT OF A POT OF HONEY, WHICH WAS so kindly taken that the god bade her ask what she would, and that it should be granted her. The Bee then desired that wherever she should set her sting it might wound to the death. Jupiter was loath to leave mankind at the mercy of a spiteful little insect, and was annoyed at the ill nature of her wish. He therefore said that while, for his promise's sake he would give her the power to harm, she must be careful how she used the power, for where she planted her sting she would leave it, and with it lose her life.

Evil brings evil in return.

THE DOGS AND THE HIDES

SOME DOGS, FAMISHED WITH HUNGER, SAW SOME COWHIDES steeping in a river. Not being able to reach them, they agreed to drink up the river: but it fell out that they burst themselves with drinking long before they reached the hides.

Attempt not impossibilities.

THE LION, THE TIGER, AND THE FOX

A LION AND A TIGER HAPPENED TO COME TOGETHER OVER THE dead body of a Fawn that had been recently shot. A fierce battle ensued, and as each animal was in the prime of his age and strength, the combat was long and furious. At last they lay stretched on the ground panting, bleeding, and exhausted, each unable to lift a paw against the other. An impudent Fox coming by at the time stepped in and carried off before their eyes the prey on account of which they had both fought so savagely. "Woe betide us," said the Lion, "that we should suffer so much to serve a Fox!"

It often happens that one has the toil and another the profit.

THE PLAYFUL ASS

AN ASS CLIMBED UP TO THE ROOF OF A BUILDING AND, FRISKING about there, broke in the tiling. The owner went up after him, and quickly drove him down, beating him severely with a thick wooden cudgel. The Ass said, "Why, I saw the Monkey do this very thing yesterday, and you all laughed heartily, as if it afforded you very great amusement."

Those who do not know their right place must be taught it.

JUPITER AND THE HERDSMAN

A HERDSMAN MISSING A YOUNG COW THAT BELONGED TO the herd went up and down the forest to seek it. Not being able to find it, he prayed to Jupiter, and promised to sacrifice a Kid if he would help him to find the thief. He then went on a little farther, and suddenly came upon a Lion, grumbling over the carcass of the Cow, and feeding upon it. "Great Jupiter!" cried the Man, "I promised thee a Kid, if thou wouldst show me the thief. I now offer thee a full-grown Bull, if thou wilt mercifully deliver me safe from his clutches."

The fulfillment of our wishes might lead to ruin.

THE ASS, THE DOG, AND THE WOLF

A LADEN ASS WAS JOGGING ALONG, FOLLOWED BY HIS TIRED Master, at whose heels came a hungry Dog. Their path lay across a meadow, and the Man stretched himself out on the turf and went to sleep. The Ass fed on the pasture, and was in no hurry at all to move. The Dog alone, being gnawed by the pangs of hunger, found that the time passed heavily. "Pray, dear companion," said he to the Ass, "stoop down, that I may take my dinner from the pannier." The Ass turned a deaf ear, and went on cropping away the green and tender grass. The Dog persisted, and at last the Ass replied, "Wait, can't you, till our master wakes. He will give you your usual portion, without fail." Just then a famished Wolf appeared upon the scene, and sprang at the throat of the Ass. "Help, help, dear Towzer!" cried the Ass; but the Dog would not budge. "Wait till our Master wakes," said he; "he will come to your help, without fail." The words were no sooner spoken, than the Ass lay strangled upon the sod.

Favors beget favors.

THE ANGLER
AND THE
LITTLE FISH

A FISHERMAN WHO HAD CAUGHT
a very small Fish was about to
throw him into his basket. The
little fellow, gasping, pleaded thus
for his life: "What! you are never
going to keep such a Minnow as
I am, not one-quarter grown! Fifty like me wouldn't
make a decent dish. Do throw me back, and come

and catch me again when I am bigger." "It's all very well to say 'Catch me again,' my little fellow," replied the Man, "but you know you'll make yourself very scarce for the future. You're big enough now to make one in a frying-pan, so in you go."

*No **time like the present.***

THE CAT AND THE SPARROWS

A GREAT FRIENDSHIP ONCE EXISTED BETWEEN A SPARROW AND A Cat, to whom, when quite a kitten, the bird had been given. When they were playing together, the bold Sparrow would often fly into little mimic rages, and peck the Cat with his bill, while Pussy would beat him off with only half-opened claws; and though this sport would often wax warm, there was never real anger between them. It happened, however, that the bird made the acquaintance of another Sparrow, and being both of them saucy fellows, they soon fell out and quarreled in earnest. The little friend of the Cat, in these fights, generally fared the worst; and one day he came trembling all over with passion, and besought the Cat to avenge his wrongs for him. Pussy thereupon pounced on the offending stranger, and speedily crunched him up and swallowed him. "I had no idea before that Sparrows were so nice," said the Cat to herself, for her blood was now stirred; and as quick as thought her little playmate was seized and sent to join his enemy.

Trouble is more easily started than stopped.

THE DOG IN THE MANGER

A Dog was lying in a manger full of hay. An Ox, being hungry, came near and was going to eat of the hay. The Dog, getting up and snarling at him, would not let him touch it. "Surly creature," said the Ox, "you cannot eat the hay yourself, and yet you will let no one else have any."

Do not begrudge others what you yourself cannot enjoy.

THE FLYING-FISH AND THE DOLPHIN

A Flying-Fish, being pursued by a Dolphin, swam for safety into shallow water. Seeing the Dolphin still after him, he came too far into shore and was thrown by the waves high and dry on the sand. The Dolphin, eager in pursuit, and unable to stop himself, was also stranded. The Flying-Fish, beholding the Dolphin in the same condition as himself, said, "Now I die with pleasure, for I see my enemy has met the same fate."

Revenge is sweet.

THE GOOSE AND THE SWANS

A vain and empty Goose one day complained shrilly to members of her flock of the ill regard given Geese compared to other birds. "See the Peacock, yonder," she gestured with a flap of her wing, "and how she hides her flaws behind her gaudy feathers. Were she and I stripped, I pledge my word that all would find me the finer bird." Crossing the mead to where a bunch of Swans sported in the stream, she continued her tirade. "Again, what arrogance we see," she cackled, indicating the Swans. "Because we Geese are known to skim the waters delicately, these base creatures think to mimic us with their awkward and noisy splashing." So saying, she plunged into the water and, spreading her plumes, tried to assume the Swan's stately crest. "Conceited thing, elate with pride," complained one of Swans. "Though you put on airs, your oafishness reveals you to be just a silly Goose."

Foppery is the pride of fools.

THE MAN AND THE TREES

One day a Man went into a forest and asked the Trees if they would be so good as to give him a handle for his axe. The Trees readily granted his request and gave him a piece of tough Ash. But no sooner had the Man fitted it into his axe head, than he quickly began to use it, and laid about him so vigorously that the giants of the Forest fell under his strokes. "Alas!" said a doomed Oak to a Cedar, "the first step lost us all. If we had not given up our rights to the Ash, we might have stood for ages."

Let not your conduct furnish a handle against yourself.

THE WOLVES AND THE SHEEP

Once upon a time, the Wolves sent an embassy to the Sheep, desiring that there might be a lasting peace between them. "Why," said the messengers, "should we be forever at war? These wicked Dogs are the cause of it all; they are always barking at us and making us mad. Now if you will give up your Dogs, we will send you our children as hostages of peace." The silly Sheep agreed to the proposal and dismissed the Dogs. The Wolves gave up their whelps. But the young Wolves cried for their mothers, and the Wolves then claimed that the peace had been broken, and set upon the Sheep, who, deprived of their defenders, the Dogs, could make no resistance, but fell an easy prey to their enemies.

Make no truce with a sworn enemy.

THE FOX AND THE CROW

A CROW, HAVING STOLEN A PIECE OF cheese from a cottage window, flew with it to a tree that was some way off. A Fox, drawn by the smell of the cheese, came and sat at the foot of the tree, and tried to find some way of making it his. "Good morning, dear Miss Crow," said he. "How well you are looking today! What handsome feathers yours are, to be sure! Perhaps, too, your voice is as sweet as your feathers are fine. If so, you are really the Queen of Birds." The Crow, quite beside herself to hear such praise, at once opened a wide beak to let the Fox judge of her voice, and so let fall the cheese. The Fox snapped it up, and exclaimed, "Ah! ah! my good soul, learn that all who flatter have their own ends in view. That lesson will well repay you for a bit of cheese."

Beware the flatterer.

THE ASS AND THE LION HUNTING

THE LION ONCE TOOK A FANCY TO GO HUNTING IN COMPANY with an Ass. He sent the Ass into the forest, and told him to bray there as hard as he could. "By that means," said he, "you will rouse all the beasts in the forest. I shall stand here, and catch all that fly this way." So the Ass brayed in his most hideous manner;  and when the Lion was tired of slaughter, he called to him to come out of the wood. "Did I not do my part well?" asked the conceited beast. "Excellently," replied the Lion. "Had I not known that you were nothing more than an Ass, I should have been frightened myself."

The braggart is not the fighter.

THE THIEF AND HIS MOTHER

A LITTLE BOY WHO WENT TO SCHOOL STOLE ONE OF HIS SCHOOL-fellow's books and took it home. His Mother, so far from correcting him, took the book and sold it, and gave him an apple for his pains. In the course of time the Boy became a Thief, and at last was tried for his life and condemned. He was led to the gallows, a great crowd of people following, and among them his Mother, weeping bitterly. Seeing her, he prayed the officers to grant him the favor of a few parting words with her, and his request was freely granted. He went to his Mother, put his arm round her neck, and making as though he would whisper something in her ear, bit it off. Her cry of pain drew everybody's eyes upon them, and great was the indignation, that at such a time he should add another violence to his list of crimes. "Nay, good people," said he, "do not be deceived. My first theft was of a book, which I gave to my Mother. Had she whipped me for it, instead of praising me, I should not have come to the gallows now that I am a man."

Spare the rod, spoil the child.

THE ENVIOUS AND THE COVETOUS

TWO MEN, ONE A COVETOUS FELLOW AND THE OTHER THOROUGHLY possessed by the passion of envy, came together to present their petitions to Jupiter. The god sent Apollo to deal with their requests. Apollo told them that whatsoever should be granted to the first who asked, the other should receive double. The Covetous Man forbore to speak, waiting in order that he might receive twice as much as his companion. The Envious Man, in the spitefulness of his heart, thereupon prayed that one of his own eyes might be put out, knowing that the other would have to lose both of his.

Envy shoots at another and wounds itself.

THE VAIN JACKDAW

A DISCONTENTED JACKDAW once found some feathers which had fallen from the Peacocks, and dressed himself with his picked-up plumage. Then he sought out the company of these birds, and strutted about with them, much pleased with his looks. But they soon found him out, pulled their feathers off him, and treated him so roughly that he was glad to flee from them. He went back to the society of his fellow Jackdaws, but they in turn would have nothing to do with so sorry looking a bird.

The honest man shuns pretension.

THE GOAT AND THE LION

THE LION, SEEING A GOAT SKIPPING ABOUT IN HIGH GLEE UPON a steep craggy rock, called to him to come down upon the green pasture where he would be able to feed in much greater comfort. The Goat, who saw through the design of the Lion, replied, "Many thanks for your advice, dear Lion, but I wonder whether you are thinking more of my comfort, or how you would relish a nice morsel of Goat's flesh."

*Those who use trickery should not be surprised
when it does not work.*

THE SHEEP AND THE DOG

THE SHEEP ONE DAY COMPLAINED TO THE SHEPHERD THAT while they were shorn of their fleece, and their young ones often taken and killed for food, they received nothing in return but the green herbage of the earth, which grew of itself, and cost him no pains to procure. "On the other hand, your Dog," said they, "which gives no wool, and is of no use for food, is petted and fed with as good meat as his master." "Peace, bleating simpletons!" replied the Dog, who overheard them; "were it not that I look after and watch you, and keep off Wolves and thieves, small good would be to you your herbage or anything else."

Each has his allotted labor.

THE OLD MAN
AND HIS SONS

AN OLD MAN HAD SEVERAL SONS, WHO WERE ALWAYS FALLING out with one another. He had often, but to no purpose, exhorted them to live together in harmony. One day he called them round him, and producing a bundle of sticks, bade them try each in turn to break it across. Each put forth all his strength, but the bundle resisted their efforts. Then, cutting the cord which bound the sticks together, he told his Sons to break them separately. This was done with the greatest ease. "See, my Sons," exclaimed he, "the power of unity! Bound together by brotherly love, you may defy almost every mortal ill; divided, you will fall prey to your enemies."

A house divided against itself cannot stand.

THE FOX AND THE COCK

A Fox, passing early one summer's morning near a farm-yard, was caught in a trap which the farmer had planted there for that purpose. A Cock saw at a distance what had happened, and hardly daring to trust himself too near so dangerous a foe, approached him cautiously and peeped at him, not without considerable fear. The Fox saw him, and in his most bewitching manner addressed him as follows: "See, dear cousin," said he, "what an unfortunate accident has befallen me here! and, believe me, it is all on your account. I was creeping through yonder hedge, on my way homeward, when I heard you crow, and resolved, before I went any farther, to come and ask after your health. On the way I met with this disaster. Now if you would but run to the house and bring me a pointed stick, I think I could force it into this trap and free myself from its grip. Such a service, believe me, I should not soon forget." The Cock ran off and soon came back, not without the stick. But it was carried in the hand of the sturdy farmer, to whom he had told the story, and who lost no time in putting it out of Master Fox's power to do any harm for the future.

Use discrimination in your charities.

THE SENSIBLE ASS

AN OLD FELLOW, IN TIME OF WAR, WAS ALLOWING HIS ASS TO FEED in a green meadow, when he was alarmed by a sudden advance of the enemy. He tried every means in his power to urge the Ass to fly, but in vain. "The enemy are upon us," said he. "And what will the enemy do?" asked the Ass. "Will they put two pairs of panniers on my back, instead of one?" "No," answered the Man, "there is no fear of that." "Why then," replied the Ass, "I'll not stir an inch. I am born to be a slave, and my greatest enemy is he who gives me most to carry."

Conquest has no terror for slaves.

THE CREAKING WHEEL

A COACHMAN HEARING ONE OF THE WHEELS OF HIS COACH make a great noise, and perceiving that it was the worst one of the four, asked how it came to take such a liberty. The Wheel answered that from the beginning of time grumbling had always been the privilege of the weak.

Much smoke, little fire.

THE FARMER AND HIS SONS

A CERTAIN FARMER, LYING AT THE POINT OF DEATH, CALLED HIS Sons around him, and gave into their charge his fields and vineyards, telling them that a treasure lay hidden somewhere in them, within a foot of the surface of the ground. His Sons thought he spoke of money that he had hidden, and after he was buried, they dug most industriously all over the estate, but found nothing. The soil being so well loosened, however, the succeeding crops were of unequalled richness, and the Sons then found out what their Father had in view in telling them to dig for hidden treasure.

Industry is Fortune's right hand.

THE YOUNG MAN
AND HIS CAT

A YOUNG MAN BECAME SO FOND OF HIS
Cat that he made her his constant companion, and used to declare that if she were
a woman he would marry her. Venus, at
length, seeing how sincere was his affection, gratified his wishes, and changed the
Cat into a young and beautiful Woman.
The Young Man was delighted, and lost
no time in marrying her. They lived happily together until one day when the Bride
heard a Mouse in the room. Quickly springing up, she caught the Mouse, and killed it.
Venus, angry at this behavior, and seeing
that under the form of a Woman there was still hidden the
nature of a Cat, determined that form and nature should
no longer disagree, and changed her back again to a Cat.

The true nature, though hidden, will assert itself.

THE OLD WOMAN AND HER MAIDS

A CERTAIN OLD WOMAN HAD SEVERAL Maids, whom she used to call to their work every morning at the crowing of the Cock. The Maids, finding it grievous to have their sweet sleep disturbed so early, killed the Cock, thinking when he was quiet they should enjoy their warm beds a little longer. But the Old Woman, no longer knowing what time it was, woke them up thereafter in the middle of the night.

Beware of falling from bad to worse.

THE KID AND THE WOLF

A KID, SAFELY PERCHED upon a high rock, bestowed all manner of abuse upon a Wolf on the ground below. After he had called him all the evil names he could think of, the Wolf, looking up, replied, "Do not think, foolish youngster, that you annoy me. I regard the ill language as coming not from you, but from the place upon which you stand."

The best answer
for silly pretenders
is disdain.

THE ONE-EYED DOE

A Doe that had but one eye used to graze near the sea, so that she might keep her blind eye towards the water, while with the good eye she surveyed the country and saw that no hunters came near. It happened, however, that some men in a boat saw her, and as she did not perceive their approach, they came close enough to wound her. In her dying agony she cried out, "Alas, hard fate! that I should receive my death-wound from the side whence I expected no ill, and be safe on that where I looked for most danger."

Guard well the strong places.

THE OAK AND THE REEDS

A VIOLENT STORM UPROOTED AN OAK THAT GREW ON THE BANK of a river. The Oak drifted across the stream and lodged among some Reeds. Wondering to find these still standing, he could not help asking them how it was they had escaped the fury of a storm which had torn him up by the roots. "We bent our heads to the blast," said they, "and it passed over us. You stood stiff and stubborn till you could stand no longer."

Stoop to conquer.

THE RICH MAN AND THE TANNER

A RICH MAN TOOK UP HIS RESIDENCE NEXT DOOR TO A TANNER, and found the smell of the tan-yard so extremely unpleasant that he told him he must go. The Tanner delayed his departure, and the Rich Man had to speak to him several times about it; and every time the Tanner said he was making arrangements to move very shortly. This went on for some time, till at last the Rich Man got so used to the smell that he ceased to mind it, and troubled the Tanner with his objections no more.

Minor annoyances lessen with time.

THE GNAT AND THE LION

"I am not afraid of you," once said the Gnat to the Lion. "You may be stronger than I, but I can conquer you, and all your cruel claws and sharp teeth will avail you nothing against my sting. Let us fight it out, here and now." Having sounded his buzzing challenge, he at once attacked the Lion, whom he so enraged by stinging the most sensitive parts of his nose, eyes, and ears, that the beast roared in anguish, and, maddened with pain, tore himself cruelly with his claws. All the attempts of the Lion to crush the Gnat were in vain, and the insect returned again and again to the charge. At last the poor beast lay exhausted and bleeding upon the ground. The Gnat, hovering over the spot, and sounding a note of triumph, happened to come in the way of the web of a Spider which, slight as it was, was enough to stop him in his career. His efforts to escape only fixed him more firmly in the toils, and he who had vanquished the Lion became the prey of the Spider.

Victory is not always lasting.

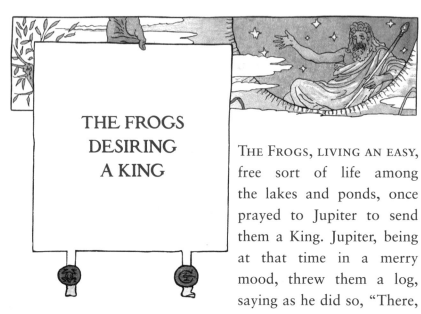

THE FROGS DESIRING A KING

THE FROGS, LIVING AN EASY, free sort of life among the lakes and ponds, once prayed to Jupiter to send them a King. Jupiter, being at that time in a merry mood, threw them a log, saying as he did so, "There, then, is a King for you." Awed by the splash, the Frogs watched their King in fear and trembling, till at last, encouraged by his stillness, one more daring than the rest jumped upon the shoulder of his monarch. Soon, many others followed his example, and made merry on the back of their unresisting King. Speedily tiring

of such a torpid ruler, they again petitioned Jupiter, and asked him to send them something more like a King. This time he sent them a Stork, who chased them about and gobbled them up as fast as he could. They lost no time, therefore, in beseeching the god to give them again their former state. "No, no," replied he; "a King that did you no harm did not please you. Make the best of the one you have, or you may chance to get a worse in his place."

Let well enough alone.

THE OLD TROUT, THE YOUNG TROUT, AND THE SALMON

A FISHERMAN, IN THE MONTH OF MAY, STOOD ANGLING ON THE bank of a river with an artificial fly. He threw his bait with so much art that a Young Trout was rushing towards it, when she was prevented by her mother. "Stop, child!" said she, "never be too hasty where there is a possibility of danger. Take due time to consider, before you risk an action that may be fatal. How do you know whether that is indeed a fly, or the snare of an enemy? Let someone else make the experiment before you. If it be a fly, he will very probably elude the first attack, and then the second may be made, if not with success, at least with safety." She had no sooner uttered this caution than a Salmon seized upon the pretended fly, and was captured.

Do not rush into a strange position.

THE HORSE
AND THE ASS

A WARHORSE, GAILY CAPARISONED, WITH ARCHING NECK AND lofty tread, the ground ringing beneath his hoofs, overtook a patient Ass, slowly walking along under a heavy load. "Out of my way!" cried the Horse in a haughty tone, "and give me room to pass." The poor Ass did as he was told, sighing at the inequality of their lots. Not long after, he met the same Horse near the same spot; but in how different circumstances! Wounded in battle, and his Master killed, he was now lame, half blind, heavily laden, and driven with many blows by a brutal carrier, into whose hands he had fallen.

Pride goes before a fall.

HERCULES AND THE WAGONER

AS A WAGONER WAS DRIVING his team through a miry lane, the wheels stuck fast in the clay, and the Horses could get on no further. The Man dropped on his knees, and began crying and praying to Hercules with all his might to come and help him. "Lazy fellow!" said Hercules, "get up and stir yourself. Whip your Horses stoutly, and put your shoulder to the wheel. If you want my help then, you shall have it."

Heaven helps those who help themselves.

THE SHEPHERD AND THE YOUNG WOLF

A SHEPHERD FOUND THE YOUNG CUB OF A WOLF, AND CAUSED IT to be brought up among his Dogs, with whom it grew to be quite friendly. When any other Wolves came, meaning to rob the fold, this young fellow was among the foremost to give them chase, but on returning he generally managed to linger behind the Dogs, and keep a sharp lookout for any stray Sheep from the fold. Instead, however, of bringing these home, he would drive them to an out-of-the-way spot, and there mangle and partially devour them. He did this once too often, and was caught at it by the Shepherd, who hung him by the neck from the bough of a tree, and in that way put an end to his double-dealing.

Double-dealing is worse than open enmity.

THE LION AND THE ELEPHANT

THE LION COMPLAINED MOST SADLY THAT A BEAST WITH SUCH claws, teeth, and strength as he possessed, should yet be moved to a state of abject terror at the crowing of a Cock. "Can life be worth having," said he, "when so vile a creature has the power to rob it of its charms?" Just then, a huge Elephant came along, flapping his ears quickly to and fro, with an air of great concern. "What troubles you so?" said the Lion to the Elephant. "Can any mortal thing have power to harm a beast so large as you?" "Do you see this little buzzing Gnat?" replied the Elephant; "let him

but sting the inner part of my ear, and I shall go mad with pain." The Lion thereupon took heart again, and determined not to let troubles, which he shared in common with all created things, blind him to what was pleasant in life.

Brooding over troubles increases them.

THE DEER AND THE LION

A Deer, being hard pressed by the Hounds, found a cave into which he rushed for safety. An immense Lion, couched at the farther end of the cave, sprang upon him in an instant. "Unhappy creature that I am!" exclaimed the Deer, in his dying moments. "I entered this cave to escape the pursuit of Men and Dogs, and I have fallen into the jaws of the most terrible of wild beasts."

In avoiding one evil, plunge not into a worse.

THE LION AND THE EAGLE

An Eagle stayed his flight, and entreated a Lion to make an alliance with him to their mutual advantage. The Lion replied, "I have no objection, but you must excuse me for requiring you to find surety for your good faith; for how can I trust any one as a friend, who is able to fly away from his bargain whenever he pleases?"

Try before you trust.

THE LION AND THE BULL

A LION, GREATLY DESIROUS TO CAPTURE A BULL AND YET AFRAID to attack him on account of his great size, resorted to a trick to ensure his destruction. He approached him and said, "I have slain a fine Sheep, my friend; and if you will come home and partake of him with me, I shall be delighted to have your company." The Lion said this in the hope that, as the Bull was in the act of reclining to eat, he might attack him to advantage, and make his meal on him. The Bull, however, on his approach to the den, saw the huge spits and giant cauldrons, and no sign whatever of the Sheep, and, without saying a word, quietly took his departure. The Lion inquired why he went off so abruptly without a word of salutation to his host, who had not given him any cause of offense. "I have reasons enough," said the Bull. "I see no indication whatever of your having slaughtered a Sheep, while I do see, very plainly, every preparation for your dining on a Bull."

Forewarned is forearmed.

THE OAK AND THE WILLOW

A CONCEITED WILLOW HAD ONCE THE VANITY TO CHALLENGE his mighty neighbor, the Oak, to a trial of strength. It was to be determined by the next storm, and Aeolus was addressed by both parties, to exert his most powerful efforts. This was no sooner asked than granted; and a violent hurricane arose. The pliant

Willow, bending from the blast, or shrinking under it, evaded all its force; while the generous Oak, disdaining to give way, opposed its fury, and was torn up by the roots. Immediately the Willow began to exult, and to claim the victory; when thus the fallen Oak interrupted his exultation: "Callest thou this a trial of strength? Poor wretch! not to thy strength, but weakness; not to thy boldly facing danger, but meanly skulking from it, thou owest thy present safety. I am an Oak, though fallen; thou still a Willow, though unhurt; but who, except so mean a wretch as thyself, would prefer an ignominious life, preserved by craft or cowardice, to the glory of meeting death in a brave contention?"

The courage of meeting death in an honorable cause is more commendable than any address or artifice we can use to evade it.

THE ROSE AND THE AMARANTH

An Amaranth, planted in a garden near a Rosebush, thus addressed it: "What a lovely flower is the Rose, a favorite alike with gods and with men. I envy you your beauty and your perfume." The Rose replied, "I indeed, dear Amaranth, flourish but for a brief season! If no cruel hand pluck me from my stem, yet I must perish by an early doom. But you are immortal, and never fade, but bloom forever in renewed youth."

Lasting things are best.

THE LION AND
THE FROG

THE LION, HEARING AN ODD KIND OF A HOLLOW VOICE AND seeing nobody, started up. He listened again; the voice continued, and he shook with fear. At last seeing a Frog crawl out of the lake, and finding that the noise proceeded from that little creature, he crushed it to pieces with his feet.

Imaginary terrors fill a timorous soul with real fear.

E.G.

THE CORMORANT AND THE FISHES

A CORMORANT, WHOSE EYES WERE SO DIM WITH AGE THAT he could not discern his prey at the bottom of the waters, devised a trick to supply his wants. "Hark you, friend," said he to a Gudgeon, whom he found swimming near the surface of a certain canal, "if you have any regard for yourself or your brethren, go at once and tell them from me that the owner of this piece of water means to drag it a week hence." The Gudgeon immediately swam away and made his report of this terrible news to a general assembly of the fishes, who unanimously agreed to send him back as their ambassador to the Cormorant. He was to return their thanks for the intelligence, and to add their entreaties that, as he had been so good as to inform them of their danger, he would be graciously pleased to put them into the way of escaping it. "That I will, most readily," replied the artful Cormorant, "and assist you with my best services into the bargain. You have only to collect yourselves together at the top of the water, and I will undertake to transport you, one by one, to my own residence, at the side of a solitary pool, to which no creature but myself ever found the way." The project was approved by the unwary fishes, and quickly performed by the deceitful Cormorant. When he had placed them in a shallow piece of water, the bottom of which his eyes could easily discern, they were all devoured by him in their turn, as his hunger or luxury required.

*It is not wise to trust an enemy or stranger
so far as to put yourself in his power.*

THE FIR TREE AND THE BRAMBLE

THE FIR TREE TREATED WITH CONTEMPT THE BRAMBLE THAT grew at its foot. "I am put to many high and noble uses," said he boastfully. "I furnish taper spars for ships, and beams for the roofs of palaces. You are trodden under foot, and despised by everybody." "You talk very finely now," replied the Bramble; "but, for all that, when once you feel the axe applied to your root, you'll wish you had been a Bramble."

Better poverty without care than riches with care.

THE PHILOSOPHER AMONG THE TOMBS

A SAGE PHILOSOPHER, WELL VERSED IN ALL KNOWLEDGE NATUral as well as moral, was one day found in a cemetery deeply absorbed in contemplating two human skeletons which lay before him—the one that of a duke, the other that of a common beggar. After some time he made this exclamation: "If skillful anatomists have made it appear that the bones, nerves, muscles, and entrails of all men are made after the same manner and form, surely this is a most convincing proof that true nobility is situated in the mind, and not in the blood."

In death, the rich and the poor meet together.

THE HAWK AND THE NIGHTINGALE

A NIGHTINGALE ONCE FELL INTO THE CLUTCHES OF A HUNGRY Hawk who had been all day on the lookout for food. "Pray let me go," said the Nightingale, "I am such a mite for a stomach like yours. I sing so nicely, too. Do let me go, it will do you good to hear me." "Much good it will do an empty stomach," replied the Hawk, "and besides, a little bird that I have is more to me than a great one that has yet to be caught."

A bird in the hand is worth two in the bush.

THE BODY AND ITS MEMBERS

THE MEMBERS OF THE BODY ONCE REBELLED AGAINST HIM. THEY said he led an idle, lazy life at their expense. The Hands declared that they would not again lift a crust even to keep him from starving, the Mouth that it would not take in a bit more food, the Legs that they would carry him about no longer, and so on with the others. The Body quietly allowed them to follow their own courses, well knowing that they would all soon come to their senses, as indeed they did, when, for want of the blood and nourishment supplied from the stomach, they found themselves fast becoming mere skin and bone.

No one can live to himself, but must take account of his neighbors' needs.

THE CITY MOUSE AND
THE COUNTRY MOUSE

A COUNTRY MOUSE — A PLAIN, SENSIBLE SORT OF FELLOW — WAS once visited by a former friend of his, who lived in a neighboring city. The Country Mouse put before his friend some fine peas and wheat-stalks, and called upon him to eat heartily of the good cheer. The City Mouse nibbled a little here and there in a dainty manner, wondering at the pleasure his host took in such coarse and ordinary fare. Finally the City Mouse said to his host, in their after-dinner chat, "Really, my good friend, I am surprised that you can keep in such spirits in this dismal, dead-and-alive kind of place. You see here no life, no gaiety, no society in short, but go on and on, in a dull, humdrum sort of way, from one year's end to another. Come now with me this very night, and see with your own eyes what a life I lead." The Country Mouse consented, and as soon as it was dark, off they started for the city, where they arrived just at the end of a splendid supper given by the master of the house where our town friend lived. The City Mouse soon got together a heap of dainties on a corner of the handsome carpet. The Country Mouse, who had never even heard the names of half the meats set before him, was hesitating where he should begin, when the room door creaked, opened, and in entered a servant with a light. Off ran the Mice; but everything soon being quiet again, they returned to their repast, when once more the door opened, and the son of the master of the house came running in, followed by his little Terrier, who ran sniffing to the very spot where our friends had just been. The City Mouse was by that time safe in his hole — which, by the way, he had not been thoughtful

enough to show to his friend, who could find no better shelter than that afforded by a sofa, behind which he waited in fear and trembling till quiet was again restored. The City Mouse then called upon him to resume his supper, but the Country Mouse said, "No, no; I shall be off as fast as I can. I would rather have my wheat-stalk with peace and security, than all your fine things in the midst of such alarms and frights as these."

A crust with quietness is better than a feast eaten in fear.

THE TORTOISE AND THE EAGLE

A Tortoise, weary of crawling about on the ground at a snail's pace, desired to fly in the air like the birds, and gave out that if any bird would take him up in the clouds and show him the world, he would tell him in return where to find treasures hid in the earth. The Eagle thereupon did as he wished, but finding that

the Tortoise could not keep his word, carried him up once more, and let him fall on a hard rock, where he was dashed to pieces.

Never make rash promises.

THE ATHENIAN AND THE THEBAN

AN ATHENIAN AND A THEBAN WERE ON THE ROAD TOGETHER, AND passed the time in conversation, as is the way of travelers. After discussing a variety of subjects they began to talk about heroes, a topic that tends to be more fertile than edifying. Each of them was lavish in his praises of the heroes of his own city, until eventually the Theban asserted that Hercules was the greatest hero who had ever lived on earth, and now occupied a foremost place among the gods; while the Athenian insisted that Theseus was far superior, for his fortune had been in every way supremely blessed, whereas Hercules had at one time been forced to act as a servant. And he gained his point, for he was a very glib fellow, like all Athenians; so that the Theban, who was no match for him in talking, cried at last in some disgust, "All right, have your way; I only hope that, when our heroes are angry with us, Athens may suffer from the anger of Hercules, and Thebes only from that of Theseus."

To each his own.

THE MOUNTAIN IN LABOR

IN OLDEN TIMES, A MIGHTY RUMBLING WAS HEARD IN A MOUN-tain. This lasted a long time, until all the country round about was shaken. The people flocked together, from far and near, to see what would come of the upheaval. After many days of waiting and wise prophesyings from the crowd—out came a Mouse.

Do not make much ado about nothing.

THE CROW AND THE RAVEN

A CROW WAS VERY JEALOUS OF THE RAVEN, BECAUSE HE WAS considered a bird of good omen, and always attracted the attention of men, as indicating by his flight the good or evil course of future events. Seeing some travelers approaching, she flew up into a tree, and perching herself on one of the branches, cawed as loudly as she could. The travelers turned towards the sound, and wondered what it boded, when one of them said to his companion, "Let us proceed on our journey, my friend, for it is only the caw of a Crow, and her cry, you know, is no omen."

Those who assume a character that does not belong to them only make themselves ridiculous.

THE ASS LADEN WITH SALT AND SPONGES

A MAN DROVE HIS ASS TO THE SEASIDE, AND HAVING PURCHASED there a load of salt, proceeded on his way home. In crossing a stream the Ass stumbled and fell. It was some time before he regained his feet, and by that time the Salt had all melted away, and he was delighted to find that he had lost his burden. A little while after that, the Ass, when laden with sponges, had occasion to cross the same stream. Remembering his former good luck, he stumbled this time on purpose, and was surprised to find that his load, so far from disappearing, became many times heavier than before.

The same ploy does not often succeed twice.

THE ASS EATING THISTLES

AN ASS LADEN WITH VERY CHOICE PROVISIONS, WHICH HE WAS carrying in harvest-time to the field for his master and the reapers, stopped by the way to eat a large and strong thistle that grew by the roadside. "Many people would wonder," said he, "that with such delicate viands within reach, I do not touch them; but to me this bitter and prickly thistle is more savory and relishing than anything else in the world."

What is one man's poison is another man's meat.

THE BEGGAR AND HIS DOG

A Beggar and his Dog sat at the gate of a noble Courtier, and were preparing to make a meal on a bowl of fragments
that had been brought out by the kitchen-maid. A poor
dependent of his Lordship's, who had been sharing the singular favor of a dinner at the steward's table, was struck with the
appearance, and stopped a little to observe them. The Beggar,
hungry and voracious as any courtier in Christendom, seized with
greediness the choicest morsels and swallowed them himself; the
residue was divided into portions for his children. A scrap was
thrust into one pocket for honest Jack, a crust into another for
bashful Tom, and a luncheon of cheese was wrapped up with care
for the little favorite of his hopeful family. In short, if anything
was thrown to the Dog, it was a bone so closely picked that it
scarce afforded a pittance to keep life and soul together. "How
exactly alike," said the dependent, "is this poor Dog's case and
mine! He is watching for a dinner from a Master who cannot
spare it; I for a place from a needy Lord whose wants, perhaps,

are greater than my own, and whose relations are more clamorous than any of this Beggar's brats."

'Tis misery to depend upon patrons whose circumstances
make their charity necessary at home.

THE WOLF IN DISGUISE

A WOLF, WHO BY HIS FREQUENT VISITS TO A FLOCK OF SHEEP IN his neighborhood began to be extremely well known to them, thought it expedient, for the more success-fully carrying on of his depredations, to appear in a new character. To this end, he disguised himself in a shepherd's habit; and, resting his forefeet upon a stick, which served him by way of crook, he softly made his approach toward the fold. It happened that the Shepherd and his Dog were both of them extended on the grass, fast asleep, so that he would certainly have succeeded in his project, if he had not imprudently attempted to imitate the Shepherd's voice. The horrid noise awakened them both; and the Wolf, encumbered with his disguise, and finding it impossible either to resist or to flee, yielded up his life an easy prey to the Shepherd's Dog.

Hypocrites frequently lay themselves
open to discovery by overacting their parts.

THE COUNCIL OF HORSES

Once upon a time, a brash young Colt dissatisfied with the lot of his kind complained loudly to the Council of Horses: "How abject is our race! Are we condemned to slavery and servitude because our sires so willingly bore the chain? Is it right that Men should exploit our strength? Were we created only to serve their needs—dragging their plowshares, sweating in their harnesses, groaning beneath the loads they pile upon our backs? Reject the rein and spurn the spur! Let us be like the lion and the tiger and assert our claim to freedom and independence." Neighs of assent broke out among the assembled horses, and there was a great pawing of the ground in applause. But all were silenced when a Steed of great age and long experience addressed the assembly thus: "When I had the health and strength of my youth, I toiled as you do. Now, my grateful owner rewards my past pains by allowing me to roam freely and to feed on the crops yielded by the fields I once plowed. It is true that Man expects us to lend our pains to his endeavors, but does he not divide his care through all our labors of the year? Does he not provide us with buildings to shield us from the inclement weather and to keep our hay dry? Does he not share with us the bounty of the harvest? Since it is decreed that all creatures should help one another, ought we not be happy with our lot?" Seeing the wisdom of what their elder said, the Horses previously fired by the young Colt's discontent agreed, and the tumult ceased.

Those who know their station in life know the greatest contentment.

THE SOW AND THE WOLF

A Sow lay one day in the sty with her whole litter of pigs about her. A Wolf who longed for a small porker, but knew not how to get it, tried to worm himself into the good opinion of the mother. "How do you find yourself today, Mrs. Sow?" said he. "A little fresh air would certainly do you great good. Now, do go abroad and air yourself a little, and I will gladly mind your children till you return." "Many thanks for your offer," replied the Sow. "I know very well what kind of care you would take of my little ones, but if you really wish to be as obliging as you pretend to be, you will not show me your face again."

Services from strangers are to be suspected.

THE TRUMPETER
TAKEN PRISONER

Upon the defeat of an army in battle, a Trumpeter was taken prisoner. The Soldiers were about to put him to death, when he cried, "Nay, gentlemen, why should you kill me? This baud of mine is guiltless of a single life." "Yes," replied the Soldiers; "but with that braying instrument of yours you incite others, and you must share the same fate as they."

Those who aid are as guilty as those who do evil.

MINERVA AND THE OWL

"My most solemn and wise bird," said Minerva one day to her Owl. "Having hitherto admired you for your profound taciturnity, I have now a mind for variety to have you display your parts in discourse; for silence is only admirable in one who can, when he pleases, triumph by his eloquence and charm with graceful conversation." The Owl replied by solemn grimaces, and made dumb signs. Minerva bid him lay aside that affectation and begin; but he only shook his wise head and remained silent. Whereupon Minerva, provoked with this mimicry of wisdom, commanded him to speak immediately, on pain of her displeasure. The Owl, seeing no remedy, drew up close to Minerva, and whispered very softly in her ear this sage remark: "Since the world has grown so depraved, they ought to be esteemed most wise who have eyes to see and wit to hold their tongues."

Silence sometimes speaks louder
than words.

THE LION AND THE MOUSE

A Lion, tired with the chase, lay sleeping at full length under a shady tree. Some Mice, scrambling over him while he slept, awoke him. Laying his paw upon one of them, he was about to crush him, when the Mouse implored his mercy. "Spare me, O

King!" said he, "and maybe the day will come when I can be of service to you." The Lion, tickled with the idea of the Mouse helping him, lifted his paw and let the little creature go. Some time after, the Lion was caught in a net laid by some hunters, and, unable to free himself, made the forest resound with his roars. The Mouse whose life had been spared came, and with his little sharp teeth soon gnawed the ropes asunder, and set the Lion free.

The least may help the greatest.

HERCULES AND PLUTUS

WHEN HERCULES WAS RAISED TO THE DIGNITY OF A GOD, AND took his place on Olympus, he went round and paid his respects to all the gods and goddesses, excepting only Plutus, the God of Wealth, to whom he made no sign. This caused much astonishment, and Jupiter, at the first favorable opportunity, asked Hercules for an explanation. "Why," answered he, "I have seen that god in the company of such rascals when on earth, that I did not know whether it would be considered reputable to be seen talking to him in heaven."

Wealth and respectability are often at variance.

THE SHEPHERD TURNED MERCHANT

A SHEPHERD WHO KEPT HIS SHEEP AT NO GREAT DISTANCE FROM the sea one day drove them close to the shore, and sat down on a rock to enjoy the cool breeze. It was a beautiful summer day, and the ocean lay before him, calm, smooth, and of an enchanting blue. As he watched the white sails, and listened to the measured plash of the tiny wavelets on the pebbled beach, his heart thrilled with pleasure. "How happy," exclaimed he, "should I be if, in a tight, trim bark of my own, with wings like a bird, I could skim that lovely plain, visit other lands, see other peoples, and become rich in ministering to their wants and pleasures!" He sold his flock, and all that he had, bought a small ship, loaded her with dates, and set sail. A storm arose: the cargo was thrown overboard to lighten the ship, but in spite of all efforts she was driven upon a rock near the shore, and went to pieces. The Shepherd narrowly escaped with his life, and was afterwards glad to earn his bread by watching the flock which had formerly been his own. In the course of time, when, by care and frugality, he had again become possessed of some amount of wealth, he happened to find himself sitting on the self-same rock, and on just such another lovely day as that on which he had resolved to become a Merchant. The sea lapped temptingly on the beach at his feet. "Foolish sea!" the Shepherd cried, "do you think I am ass enough to try you a second time? You want some more dates, do you?"

Experience is a sure teacher.

THE CAT AND THE FOX

THE CAT AND THE FOX WERE ONCE TALK-ing together in the middle of a forest. "Let things be never so bad," said the Fox, "I don't care; I have a hundred tricks to escape my enemies, if one should fail." "I," replied the Cat, "have but one; if that fails me, I am undone." "I am sorry for you," said the Fox. "You are truly to be pitied; and if you were not such a helpless creature, I'd give you one or two of my tricks. As it is, I suppose each must shift for himself." Just then a pack of Hounds burst into view. The Cat, having recourse to her one means of defense, flew up a tree, and sat securely among the branches, from whence she saw the Fox, after trying his hundred tricks in vain, overtaken by the Dogs and torn in pieces.

One thing well learned brings safety.

THE LION AND THE FOUR BULLS

FOUR BULLS WERE SUCH GREAT FRIENDS THAT THEY ALWAYS kept together when feeding. A Lion watched them for many days with longing eyes; but never being able to find one apart from the rest, was afraid to attack them. He at length succeeded in awakening a jealousy among them, which finally became hatred, and they strayed off at some distance from each other. The Lion then fell upon them singly, and killed them all.

There is strength in unity.

THE WOLF AND THE FOX

THE WOLVES AND FOXES ONCE SELECTED ONE OF THEIR NUMBER to be their ruler. The Wolf that was chosen was a plausible, smooth-spoken rascal, and on a very early day he addressed an assembly of his subjects as follows: "One thing," he said, "is of such vital importance, and will tend so much to our general welfare, that I cannot impress it too strongly upon your attention. Nothing cherishes true brotherly feeling and promotes the general good so much as the suppression of all selfishness. Let each one of you, then, share with any hungry brother who may be near whatever in hunting may fall to your lot." "Hear, hear!" cried a Fox, who had listened to the speech; "and of course you yourself will begin with the fat Sheep that you hid yesterday in a corner of your lair."

Practice what you preach.

THE FROG AND THE MOUSE

A FROG AND A MOUSE, WHO HAD LONG BEEN RIVALS FOR THE sovereignty of a certain marsh, and had many a skirmish and running fight together, agreed one day to settle the matter, once for all, by a fair and open combat. They met, and each, armed with the point of a bulrush for a spear, was ready to fight to the death. The combat began in earnest, and there is no knowing how it might have ended, had not a Kite, seeing them from afar, pounced down and carried off both heroes in her talons.

Peace brings security.

THE HORSE AND THE GROOM

A DISHONEST GROOM REGULARLY USED TO SELL A GOOD HALF OF the measure of oats that was daily allowed for a Horse, the care of which was entrusted to him. He would, however, keepcurrying the animal for hours together, to make him appear in good condition. The Horse naturally resented this treatment. "If you really wish me to look sleek," said he, "in the future give me half the currying, and twice as much food."

There is no parleying with the dishonest.

THE OLD MAN AND DEATH

A POOR AND TOIL-WORN PEASANT, BENT WITH YEARS, AND groaning beneath the weight of a heavy faggot of firewood which he carried, sought, weary and sore-footed on a long and dusty road, to gain his distant cottage. Unable to bear the weight of his burden any longer, he let it fall by the roadside, and sitting down upon it, lamented his hard fate. What pleasure had he known since first he drew breath in this sad world? From dawn to dusk one round of ill-requited toil! At home, empty cupboards, a discontented wife, and disobedient children! He called on Death to free him from his troubles. At once the King of Terrors stood before him, and asked him what he wanted. Awed at the ghastly presence, the Old Man stammered out: "I—I—only wanted you to help me put this bundle of sticks on my shoulders again."

What is desired in fancy is often regretted in reality.

THE TRAVELERS AND THE PLANE TREE

Two Travelers, worn out by the heat of the summer's sun, laid themselves down at noon under the wide-spreading branches of a Plane Tree. As they rested under its shade, one of the Travelers said to the other, "What a singularly useless tree is the Plane! It bears no fruit, and is not of the least service to man." The Plane Tree, interrupting him, said, "You ungrateful fellow! Do you, while receiving benefits from me, and resting under my shade, dare to describe me as useless and unprofitable?"

Some men despise their best blessings.

THE COUNTRYMAN AND THE SNAKE

A Countryman, one frosty day in the depth of winter, found a Snake under a hedge almost dead with the cold. Taking pity on the poor creature, he brought it home, and laid it on the hearth near the fire. Revived by the heat, it reared itself up, and with dreadful hissings flew at the wife and children of its benefactor. The Countryman, hearing their cries, rushed in, and, seizing a mattock, soon cut the Snake in pieces. "Vile wretch!" said he; "is this the reward you make to him who saved your life? Die, as you deserve; but a single death is too good for you."

Ingratitude is a crime.

THE SICK STAG

A STAG WHOSE JOINTS HAD BECOME STIFF WITH OLD AGE WAS AT great pains to get together a large heap of fodder—enough, as he thought, to last him for the remainder of his days. He stretched himself out upon it and, now dozing, now nibbling, made up his mind to wait quietly for the end. He had always been of a gay and lively turn, and had made in his time many friends. These now came in great numbers to see him, and wish him farewell. While engaged in friendly talk over past adventures and old times, what more natural than that they should help themselves to a little of the food which seemed so plentifully stored around? The end of the matter was that the poor Stag died not so much of sickness or of old age as for sheer want of the food which his friends had eaten for him.

Thoughtless friends bring more hurt than profit.

THE SHEEP AND THE BRAMBLE

A SHEEP, DURING A SEVERE STORM, WANDERED INTO A THICKET for shelter, and there lay so snug and warm that he soon fell fast asleep. The clouds clearing away and the winds returning to rest inclined the Sheep to return to his pasture. But, ah! what was his situation: a bramble had laid such a firm hold of his fleece that it was left as a forfeit for the protection the thicket had given him.

He who makes his bed must lie in it.

THE LION AND THE HARE

A Lion came across a Hare, who lay fast asleep. He was just in the act of seizing her when a fine young Hart trotted by, and he left the Hare to follow him. The Hare, scared by the noise, awoke, and scudded away. The Lion was not able after a long chase to catch the Hart, and returned to feed upon the Hare. On finding that the Hare also had run off, he said, "I am rightly served for having let go the food I had in my hand for the chance of obtaining more."

Be content with an assured income.

THE BOY WHO CRIED WOLF

A mischievous Lad, who was set to mind some Sheep, used to cry in jest, "The Wolf! The Wolf!" When the people came running to the spot, he would laugh at them for their pains. One day the Wolf came in reality, and the Boy this time called "The Wolf! The Wolf!" in earnest; but the men, having been so often deceived, disregarded his cries, and the Sheep were left at the mercy of the Wolf.

A liar cannot be believed even when he speaks the truth.

THE OLD LION

A LION, WORN OUT WITH AGE, LAY DRAWING HIS LAST BREATH, and several of the beasts who had formerly been sufferers by him came and revenged themselves. The Boar, with his powerful tusks, ripped his flank; and the Bull gored his sides with his horns. The Ass, too, seeing there was no danger, came up and threw his heels into the Lion's face. "Alas!" groaned the dying tyrant, "how much worse than a thousand deaths it is to be spurned by so base a creature."

Respect earns respect.

THE BEES AND THEIR KEEPER

A THIEF CAME INTO A BEE GARDEN ONE DAY WHILE THE KEEPER was away and robbed the hives. Not long afterward the Keeper returned and was greatly disturbed about the theft, not only because of the loss of honey, but also because the hives had been overturned. While he was busily at work trying to set the garden at rights, the Bees came home laden from the fields and, missing their combs, flew in angry swarms about their Master. "Foolish and ungrateful creatures!" exclaimed he. "You let a stranger who has robbed you escape unharmed, while you are ready to attack your best friend."

People too often mistake their friends for their foes.

THE SATYR AND
THE TRAVELER

A Satyr, ranging in the forest in winter, came across a Traveler half starved and nearly dead with the cold. He took pity on him and invited him to go to his cave. On their way the Man kept blowing upon his fingers. "Why do you do that?" said the Satyr, who had seen little of the world. "To warm my hands; they are nearly frozen," replied the Man. Arrived at the cave, the Satyr poured out a mess of smoking pottage and laid it before the Traveler, who commenced to blow at it with

all his might. "What, blowing again!" cried the Satyr. "Is it not hot enough?" "Yes, faith," answered the Man, "it is too hot. I am blowing at it to cool it off." "Be off with you!" said the Satyr, in alarm; "I will have no part with a Man who can blow hot and cold from the same mouth."

A two-faced man makes no friends.

THE FOWLER, THE PARTRIDGE, AND THE COCK

ONE DAY, AS A FOWLER WAS SITTING DOWN TO A SCANTY SUPPER of herbs and bread, a friend dropped in unexpectedly. The larder was empty; so he went out and caught a tame Partridge, which he kept as a decoy, and was about to wring her neck when she cried, "Surely you won't kill me? Why, what will you do without me next time you go fowling? How will you get the birds to come to your nets?" He let her go at this, and went to his hen-house, where he had a plump young Cock. When the Cock saw what he was after, he too pleaded for his life, and said, "If you kill me, how will you know the time of night? and who will wake you up in the morning when it is time to get to work?" The Fowler, however, replied, "You are useful for telling the time, I know; but, for all that, I can't send my friend supperless to bed." And therewith he caught him and wrung his neck.

In times of need, people reveal their true regard for others.

THE CATS AND THE MONKEY

TWO CATS, HAVING STOLEN SOME CHEESE, COULD NOT AGREE about dividing the prize. In order, therefore, to settle the dispute, they consented to refer the matter to a Monkey. The proposed judge very readily accepted the office and, producing a balance, put a part into each scale. "Let me see," said he, "ah—this lump outweighs the other." And he bit off a considerable piece in order to make it balance. The opposite scale was now the heavier, which afforded our conscientious judge reason for a second mouthful. "Hold, hold!" said the two Cats, who began to be alarmed for the event, "give us our respective shares and we are satisfied." "If you are satisfied," returned the Monkey, "Justice is not; a cause of this nature is by no means so soon determined." He continued to nibble first one piece then the other, till the poor Cats, seeing their cheese gradually diminishing, entreated him to give himself no further trouble, but to award them what remained. "Not so fast, I beseech you, friends," replied the Monkey; "we owe Justice to ourselves as well as to you. What remains is due to me as a fee." Upon which he crammed the whole into his mouth, and with great gravity dismissed the Court.

Those who dance must pay the piper.

Ernest Griset

R.S.MARRI

THE HEN AND THE FOX

A Fox, HAVING CREPT INTO A HEN-HOUSE, looked up and down for something to eat, and at last spied a Hen sitting upon a perch so high, that he could by no means reach her. He therefore had recourse to an old stratagem. "Dear cousin," said he to her, "how do you do? I heard that you were ill, and kept at home; I could not rest, therefore, till I had come to see you. Pray let me feel your pulse. Indeed, you do not look well at all." He was running on in this impudent manner, when the Hen answered him from the roost, "Truly, dear Fox, you are in the right. I was seldom in more danger than I am now. Pray excuse my coming down; I am sure I should catch my death if I were to." The Fox, finding himself foiled, made off and tried his luck elsewhere.

Craft can be answered with craft.

THE PLAGUE AMONG THE BEASTS

A MORTAL DISTEMPER ONCE RAGED AMONG THE BEASTS, AND swept away prodigious numbers. After it had continued some time without abatement, the Beasts decided that it was a judgment inflicted upon them for their sins, and a day was appointed for a general confession; when it was agreed that he who appeared to be the greatest sinner should suffer death as an atonement for the rest. The Fox was appointed father confessor upon the occasion; and the Lion, with great generosity, condescended to be the first in making public confession. "For my part," said he, "I must acknowledge I have been an enormous offender. I have killed many innocent Sheep in my time; nay, once, but it was a case of necessity, I made a meal of the Shepherd." The Fox, with much gravity, owned that these in any other but the king, would have been inexpiable crimes; but that His Majesty had certainly a right to a few silly Sheep; nay, and to the Shepherd, too, in case of necessity. The judgment of the Fox was applauded by all the larger animals; and the Tiger, the Leopard, the Bear, and the Wolf made confession of many sins of the like nature; which were all excused with the same lenity and mercy, and their crimes accounted so venial as scarce to deserve the name of offenses. At last, a poor penitent Ass, with great contrition, acknowledged that once going through the churchyard, being very hungry and tempted by the sweetness of the grass, he had cropped a little of it, not more, however, in quantity than the tip of his tongue; he was very sorry for the misdemeanor, and hoped—"Hope!" exclaimed the Fox, with singular zeal; "what canst thou hope for after the commission of so heinous a crime? What! eat the churchyard grass! Oh,

sacrilege! This, this is the flagrant wickedness, my brethren, which has drawn the wrath of Heaven upon our heads, and this the notorious offender whose death must make atonement for all our transgressions." So saying, he ordered his entrails for sacrifice, and the Beasts went to dinner upon the rest of his carcass.

It is easy to find fault with the helpless.

SOCRATES AND HIS FRIENDS

Socrates once built a house, and everybody who saw it had something or other to say against it. "What a front!" said one. "What an inside!" said another. "What rooms! not big enough to turn round in," said a third. "Small as it is," answered Socrates, "I wish I had true friends enough to fill it."

Houses are easier to get than friends.

THE BOWMAN AND THE LION

A Man who was very skillful with his bow went up into the mountains to hunt. At his approach, there was instantly a great consternation and rout among all the wild beasts, the Lion alone showing any determination to fight. "Stop," said the Bowman to him, "and await my messenger, who has somewhat to say to you." With that, he sent an arrow after the Lion, and wounded him in the side. The Lion, smarting with anguish, fled into the depth of the thickets, but a Fox seeing him run, bade him take courage, and face his enemy. "No," said the Lion, "you will not persuade me to that; for if the messenger he sends is so sharp, what must be the power of him who sends it?"

The timid will always urge on to danger those
more valiant than themselves.

THE MASTER AND HIS SCHOLAR

As a Schoolmaster was walking upon the bank of a river, not far from his school, he heard a cry, as of someone in distress. Running to the side of the river, he saw one of his Scholars in the water, hanging by the bough of a willow. The boy, it seems, had been learning to swim with corks, and fancying that he could now do without them, had thrown them aside. The force of the stream hurried him out of his depth, and he would certainly have been drowned, had not the friendly branch of a willow hung in his way. The Master took up the corks, which were lying upon the bank, and threw them to his Scholar. "Let this be a warning to you," said he, "and in your future life never throw away your corks until you are quite sure you have strength and experience enough to swim without them."

Too great assurance is folly.

THE WIDOW AND HER SHEEP

A CERTAIN POOR WIDOW HAD ONE SOLITARY SHEEP. AT SHEAR-
ing time, wishing to take his fleece, and to avoid expense, she sheared
him herself, but used the shears so unskillfully that with the fleece she
sheared the flesh. The Sheep, writhing with pain, said: "Why do you
hurt me so, Mistress? What weight can my blood add to the wool?
If you want my flesh, there is the butcher, who will kill me in a
trice; but if you want my fleece and wool, there is the shearer,
who will shear and not hurt me."

The least outlay is not always the greatest gain.

THE LION AND THE BOAR

ON A SUMMER DAY, WHEN THE GREAT HEAT INDUCED A GENERAL
thirst, a Lion and a Boar came at the same moment to a small well
to drink. They fiercely disputed which of them should drink first,
and were soon engaged in the agonies of a mortal combat. On
their stopping to take breath for the fiercer renewal of the strife,
they saw some Vultures waiting in the distance to feast on the
one which should fall first. They at once made up their quarrel,
saying, "It is better for us to make friends, than to become the
food of Vultures."

The man at strife is always in peril.

THE MICE IN COUNCIL

A CERTAIN CAT THAT LIVED IN A LARGE COUNTRY-HOUSE WAS SO vigilant and active that the Mice, finding their numbers grievously thinned, held a council, with closed doors, to consider what they had best do. Many plans had been started and dismissed, when a young Mouse, rising and catching the eye of the president, said that he had a proposal to make, that he was sure must meet with the approval of all. "If," said he, "the Cat wore around her neck

a little bell, every step she took would make it tinkle; then, ever fore-warned of her approach, we should have time to reach our holes. By this simple means we should live in safety, and defy her power." The speaker resumed his seat with a complacent air, and a murmur of applause arose from the audience. An old gray Mouse, with a merry twinkle in his eye, now got up, and said that the plan of the last speaker was an admirable one; but he feared it had one drawback. "My young friend has not told us," said he, "who is to put the bell on the Cat."

Counsel, to be wise, must be practical.

THE GNAT AND THE BULL

A STURDY BULL WAS DRIVEN BY THE HEAT OF THE WEATHER TO wade up to his knees in a cool and swift-running stream. He had not long been there when a Gnat, who had been disporting itself in the air, pitched upon one of his horns. "My dear fellow," said the Gnat, with as great a buzz as he could manage, "pray excuse the liberty I take. If I am too heavy, only say so, and I will go at once and rest upon the poplar which grows hard by at the edge of the stream." "Stay or go, it makes no difference to me," replied the Bull. "Had it not been for your buzz, I should not even have known you were there."

Some men are more important
in their own eyes than in those of their neighbors.

THE RIVERS AND THE SEA

The Rivers joined together to complain to the Sea, saying, "Why is it that when we flow into your tides so potable and sweet, you work in us such a change, and make us salty and unfit to drink?" The Sea, perceiving that they intended to throw the blame on him, said, "Pray, cease to flow into me, and then you will not be made briny."

Some find fault with those things by which they are chiefly benefited.

THE CRAB AND THE FOX

A Crab, forsaking the seashore, chose a neighboring green meadow as its feeding ground. A Fox came across him, and being very much famished ate him up. Just as he was on the point of being eaten, the Crab said, "I well deserve my fate; for what business had I on the land, when by my nature and habits I am only adapted for the sea?"

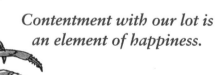

Contentment with our lot is an element of happiness.

THE NIGHTINGALE AND HIS CAGE

A NIGHTINGALE, WHICH BELONGED TO A PERSON OF QUALITY, was fed every day with plenty of choice dainties, and kept in a stately cage. Yet, notwithstanding this happy condition, he was uneasy, and envied the condition of those birds who lived free in the woods, and hopped up and down, unconfined, from bough to bough. He earnestly longed to lead the same life, and secretly pined because his wishes were denied him. After some time, however, it happened that the door of his cage was left unfastened, and the long-wished-for opportunity was given him of making his escape. Accordingly, out he flew, and hid himself among the shades of a neighboring wood, where he thought to spend the remainder of his days in contentment. But, alas! the poor bird was mistaken; a thousand evils which he never dreamed of attended this elopement of his, and he was now really that miserable creature which before he had been only in imagination. The delicate food that he used to eat was no more; he did not know how to provide for himself, and was even ready to die with hunger. A storm of rain, thunder, and lightning filled all the air, and he had no place of safety; his feathers were wetted with the heavy shower, and he was almost blinded with the flashes of lightning. His tender nature could not withstand the severe shock; he even died under it. But just before he breathed his last he is said to have made this reflection: "Ah, were I but in my cage again, I would never wander more."

Liberty is most attractive to those who
do not know its price.

THE APE AND THE BEE

AN APE, WHO, HAVING A GREAT DESIRE TO PARTAKE OF THE honey which was deposited in a rich beehive, but was intimidated from meddling with it by having felt the smart of the sting, made the following reflection: "How strange, that a Bee, while producing a delicacy so passing sweet and tempting, should also carry with him a sting so dreadfully bitter!" "Yes," answered the Bee, "equal to the sweetness of my better work is the bitterness of my sting when my anger is provoked."

Beware how you arouse the little man.

THE PASSENGER AND THE PILOT

IT HAD BLOWN A VIOLENT STORM AT SEA, AND THE WHOLE CREW of a vessel were in imminent danger of shipwreck. After the rolling of the waves was somewhat abated, a certain Passenger who had never been to sea before, observing the Pilot to have appeared wholly unconcerned, even in their greatest danger, had the curiosity to ask him what death his father died. "What death?" said the Pilot; "why, he perished at sea, as my grandfather did before him." "And are you not afraid of trusting yourself to an element that has proved thus fatal to your family?" "Afraid? by no means; why, we must all die: is not your father dead?" "Yes, but he died in his bed." "And why, then, are you not afraid of trusting yourself in your bed?" "Because I am there perfectly secure." "It may be so," replied the Pilot; "but if the hand of Providence is equally extended over all places, there is no more reason for me to be afraid of going to sea than for you to be afraid of going to bed."

Faith is not a relative matter.

THE LION AND THE ASS

A CONCEITED ASS WAS ONCE BOLD ENOUGH TO BRAY FORTH some insulting speeches against the Lion. The Lion at first began to show his teeth, but turning about and seeing who was speaking, merely remarked: "Oh, it is only the Ass!"

Contempt is the best answer for scurrility.

THE FOX AND THE LION

THE FIRST TIME THE FOX SAW THE LION HE NEARLY DIED OF fright. The next time, he gathered sufficient courage to have a good stare. The third time, he went boldly up to the Lion, and commenced a familiar conversation with him.

Familiarity breeds contempt.

THE SPARROW AND THE HARE

A HARE, BEING SEIZED BY AN EAGLE, CRIED OUT IN A PITEOUS manner. A Sparrow sitting on a tree close by, so far from pitying the poor animal, made merry at his expense. "Why did you stay there to be taken?" said he. "Could not so swift a creature as you have easily escaped from an Eagle?" Just then a Hawk swooped down and carried off the Sparrow, who, when he felt the Hawk's talons in his sides, cried still more loudly than the Hare. The Hare, in the agonies of death, received comfort from the fact that the fate of the mocking Sparrow was no better than his own.

When calamity overtakes the hard-hearted they receive no sympathy.

THE BLIND MAN AND THE WHELP

A Blind Man was accustomed to distinguishing different animals by touching them with his hands. The Whelp of a Wolf was brought him, with a request that he would feel it, and say what it was. He felt it, and being in doubt, said: "I do not quite know whether it is the Cub of a Fox, or the Whelp of a Wolf; but this I know full well, that it would not be safe to admit him to the sheep fold."

Evil tendencies are shown in early life.

THE MOUSE AND THE BULL

A Bull gave chase to a Mouse which had bitten him on the nose: but the Mouse was too quick for him and slipped into a hole in a wall. The Bull charged furiously into the wall again and again until he was tired out, and sank down on the ground exhausted with his efforts. When all was quiet, the Mouse darted out and bit him again. Beside himself with rage he started to his feet, but by that time the Mouse was back in his hole again, and he could do nothing but bellow and fume in helpless anger. Presently he heard a shrill little voice say from inside the wall, "You big fellows don't always have it your own way, you see: sometimes we little ones come off best."

The battle is not always to the strong.

THE OLD HOUND

An Old Hound, who had hunted well in his time, once seized a Stag, but from feebleness and the loss of his teeth was forced to let him go. The Master, coming up, began to beat the Old Hound cruelly, but left off when the poor animal addressed him as follows: "Hold, dear Master! You know well that neither my courage nor my will was at fault, but only my strength and my teeth, and these I have lost in your service."

Forget not past services.

THE FORTUNE-TELLER

A Man who gave himself out as a Wizard and Fortune-Teller used to stand in the marketplace and pretend to foretell the future, give information as to missing property, and other matters of the like kind. One day, while he was busily plying his trade, a waggish fellow broke through the crowd, and gasping as if for want of breath, told him that his house was in flames, and must shortly be burnt to the ground. Off ran the Wizard at the news as fast as his legs could carry him, while the Wag and a crowd of other people followed at his heels. But the house was not on fire at all; and the Wag asked him, amid the jeers of the people, how it was that he, who was so clever at telling other people's fortunes, should know so little of his own.

'Tis a poor baker who will not eat his own wares.

THE ASS AND HIS PURCHASER

A MAN WHO WANTED TO BUY AN ASS WENT TO MARKET, AND, coming across a likely-looking beast, arranged with the owner that he should be allowed to take him home on trial to see what he was like. When he reached home, he put him into his stable along with the other Asses. The newcomer took a look round, and immediately went and chose a place next to the laziest and greediest beast in the stable. When the master saw this he put a halter on him at once, and led him off and handed him over to his owner again. The latter was a good deal surprised to see him back so soon, and said, "Why, do you mean to say you have tested him already?" "I don't want to put him through any more tests," replied the other: "I could see what sort of beast he is from the companion he chose for himself."

A man is known by the company he keeps.

THE LAMB IN THE TEMPLE

A WOLF PURSUED A LAMB, WHICH FLED FOR REFUGE TO A certain temple. The Wolf called out to him and said, "The Priest will slay you in sacrifice, if he should catch you," on which the Lamb replied: "It would be better for me to be sacrificed in the temple, than to be eaten by you."

'Tis better to die for a good cause than for an evil one.

THE KITE AND THE PIGEONS

A KITE THAT HAD KEPT SAILING AROUND A DOVECOTE LOOKING for a nice fat Pigeon for many days, to no purpose, was forced by hunger to have recourse to stratagem. Approaching the Pigeons in his gentlest manner, he tried to show them how much better their state would be if they had a king with some firmness about him, and how well his protection would shield them from the attacks of the Hawk and other enemies. The Pigeons, deluded by this show of reason, admitted him to the dovecote as their king. They found, however, that he thought it part of his kingly prerogative to eat one of their number every day, and they soon repented of their credulity in having let him in. "Ah!" they exclaimed in despair; "we deserve no better. Why did we heed the counsel of an enemy?"

Trust not your security to one who puts his own interests first.

THE THIEF AND THE DOG

A THIEF WHO CAME NEAR A HOUSE ONE NIGHT TO ROB IT, WAS prevented by a Dog who began to bark loudly. The Thief tried to coax him into silence by offering him a tempting piece of meat. "No," said the Dog, "I will not sell my Master and myself for a bite of meat. For, after you have finished with him, who will take care of me?"

Honesty is the best policy.

THE FROG AND THE FOX

A FROG CAME OUT OF HIS NATIVE MARSH AND, HOPPING TO THE top of a mound of earth, gave out to all the beasts around that he was a great physician, and could heal all manner of diseases. The

Fox demanded why, if he was so clever, he did not mend his own blotched and spotted body, his stare eyes, and his lantern jaws.

Physician, heal thyself.

THE SORCERESS

NIGHT AND SILENCE HAD NOW GIVEN REPOSE TO THE WHOLE world when an old, ill-natured Sorceress, in order to exercise her infernal arts, entered into a gloomy wood that trembled at her approach. The scene of her horrid incantations was within the circumference of a large circle, in the center of which was raised an altar, where the hallowed vervain blazed in triangular flames. The mischievous Hag pronounced the dreadful words, which bound all hell in obedience to her charms. She blew a raging pestilence from her lips into the neighboring fields; the innocent cattle died, to afford a fit sacrifice to the infernal deities. The moon, by powerful spells drawn down from her orbs, entered the wood; legions of spirits from Pluto's realms appeared before the altar, and demanded her pleasure. "Tell me," said she, "where I shall find what I have lost: my favorite little dog." "How!" cried they all, enraged; "impertinent Beldame! Must the order of nature be inverted, and the repose of every creature disturbed, for the sake of thy little dog?"

*There are many people who would unhinge
the world to ease themselves of the smallest inconvenience.*

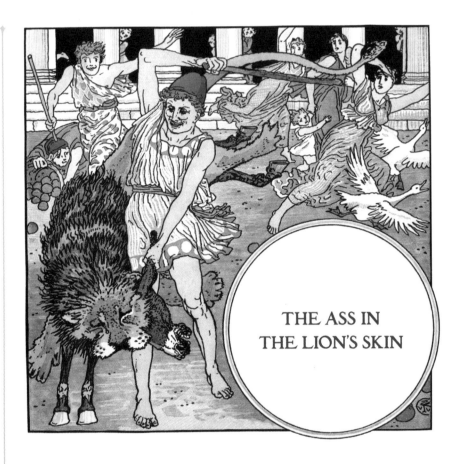

THE ASS IN THE LION'S SKIN

An Ass once found the skin of a Lion, put it on, and was highly amused to note how his presence brought terror to the other animals wherever he went. In his delight he could not resist raising his voice and braying loudly. At the sound, a Fox, who had been skulking off, turned about and said: "Ah, I thought you were a Lion, too, until I heard you bray."

Clothes do not make the man.

GENIUS, VIRTUE, AND REPUTATION

GENIUS, VIRTUE, AND REPUTATION, THREE GREAT FRIENDS, agreed to travel over the island of Great Britain, to see whatever might be worthy of observation. But as some misfortune, said they, may happen to separate us, let us consider, before we set out, by what means we may find each other again. "Should it be my ill fate," said Genius, "to be severed from my friends—heaven forbid!—you may find me kneeling in devotion before the tomb of Shakespeare; or rapt in some grove where Milton talked with angels; or musing in the grotto where Pope caught inspiration." Virtue, with a sigh, acknowledged, that her friends were not very numerous; "but were I to lose you," she cried, "with whom I am at present so happily united, I should choose to take sanctuary in the temples of religion, in the palaces of royalty, or in the stately domes of ministers of state; but as it may be my ill fortune to be there denied admittance, inquire for some cottage where contentment has a bower, and there you will certainly find me." "Ah, my dear friends," said Reputation very earnestly, "you, I perceive, when missing, may possibly be recovered; but take care, I entreat you, always to keep sight of me, for if I am once lost, I am never to be retrieved."

There are few things that can be so irreparably lost as reputation.

AESOP AND THE POULTRY

THE POPULACE OF THE NEIGHBORHOOD IN WHICH AESOP WAS a slave one day observed him attentively overlooking some poultry in an enclosure that was near the roadside; and those speculative wits who spend more time prying into other people's concerns to no purpose than in adjusting their own were moved with curiosity to know why this philosopher should bestow his attention on those animals. "I am struck," replied Aesop, "to see how mankind so readily imitates this foolish animal." "In what?" asked the neighbors. "Why, in crowing well and scraping so ill," rejoined Aesop.

It is easier by far to talk boldly and make a noisy boast of one's merits than it is to act nobly or demonstrate worth by palpable acts.

THE PORCUPINE
AND THE SNAKES

A PORCUPINE, SEEKING SHELTER, DESIRED SOME SNAKES TO GIVE him admittance into their cave. They accordingly let him in, but were afterwards so annoyed by his sharp, prickly quills, that they repented of their hospitality, and asked him to withdraw and leave them their hole to themselves. "No," said he, "you may quit the place if you don't like it; for my part, I am very well satisfied where I am."

Be cautious in your choice of friends.

HERCULES AND STRIFE

HERCULES, ONCE JOURNEYING ALONG A NARROW ROADWAY, came across a strange-looking animal that reared its head and threatened him. Undaunted, the hero gave him a few lusty blows with his club, and thought to have gone on his way. The monster however, much to the astonishment of Hercules, was now three times as big as it was before, and of a still more threatening aspect. He thereupon redoubled his blows and laid about him fast and furiously; but the harder and quicker the strokes of the club, the bigger and more frightful grew the monster, which now completely filled up the road. Pallas then appeared upon the scene. "Stop, Hercules," said she. "Cease your blows. The monster's name is Strife. Let it alone, and it will soon become as little as it was at first."

Strife increases with turmoil.

MERCURY AND THE TRAVELER

A MAN, ABOUT TO DEPART UPON A LONG JOURNEY, PRAYED TO the god Mercury, who was anciently supposed to speed Travelers, to give him good voyage and a safe return. He promised Mercury that, if he would grant his request, he would give the god half of everything he might find on his road. Soon after he set forth, he found a bag of dates and almonds, which some passerby had lost. He ate all but the stones of the dates and the shells of the almonds at once. These he laid upon a wayside altar to the god; praying him to take notice that he had kept his promise. "For," said he, "here are the insides of the one, and the outsides of the other, and that makes up your half of the booty."

A promise-breaker is never at a loss for an excuse.

THE HART
AND THE VINE

A Hart, being hard pursued by the Hunters, hid himself under the broad leaves of a shady, spreading vine. When the Hunters had gone by and given him over for lost, he thought himself quite secure, and began to crop and eat the leaves of the vine. The rustling of the branches drew the eyes of the Hunters that way, and they shot their arrows there at a venture, and killed the Hart. "I am rightly served," gasped he in dying, "for I ought not to have mistreated the friend who would have saved me."

Be not forgetful of benefits.

THE ELEPHANT AND THE
ASSEMBLY OF ANIMALS

THE WISE ELEPHANT, WHOSE EFFORTS WERE ALWAYS DIRECTED towards the benefit of his society, saw with much concern the many abuses among the Beasts, which called loudly for reform. He therefore assembled them, and, with all due respect and humility, began a long sermon, wherein he spoke plainly to them about their vices and bad habits. He called their attention especially to their idle ways; their greed, cruelty, envy, hatred, treachery, and deceit. To many of his auditors this speech was excellent and they listened with open-mouthed attention, especially such as the innocent Dove, the faithful Dog, the obedient Camel, the harmless Sheep, and the industrious Ant; the busy Bee also approved much of this lecture. Another part of the audience were extremely offended, and could scarcely endure so long an oration; the Tiger, for instance, and the Wolf were exceedingly tired, and the Serpent hissed with all his might, while a murmur of disapprobation burst from the Wasp, the Drone, the Hornet, and the Fly. The Grasshopper hopped disdainfully away from the assembly, the Sloth was indignant, and the insolent Ape mimicked the orator. The Elephant, seeing the tumult, concluded his discourse with these words: "My advice is addressed equally to all, but remember that those who feel hurt by any remarks of mine acknowledge their guilt. The innocent are unmoved."

It is the bit dog that howls.

WHITEHEAD SC

Ernest Griset

THE GARDENER AND HIS MASTER

IN THE MIDST OF A BEAUTIFUL FLOWER GARDEN THERE WAS A large pond filled with carp, tench, perch, and other freshwater fish; it was also intended to water the garden. The foolish Gardener, being particularly careful of the flowers, so emptied the pond of its water that there scarcely remained sufficient to keep the fish alive. His Master, coming down to walk in the garden, and seeing this mismanagement, scolded the Gardener, saying, "Though I am very fond of flowers, I also like to regale myself with fish." The Gardener, being a coarse, ignorant peasant, obeyed his master so precisely that he gave no water to the flowers, in order that the fish might have enough. Some time after the Master again visited his garden, and, to his great mortification, saw his beautiful flowers all dead or drooping. "You blockhead!" he cried; "in the future remember not to use so much water for the flowers as to leave me without fish, nor yet be so liberal to the fish as to kill my beauteous blossoms."

Moderation in everything is best.

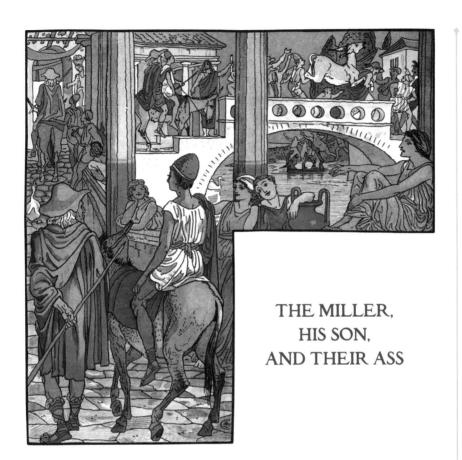

THE MILLER,
HIS SON,
AND THEIR ASS

A MILLER AND HIS SON WERE DRIVING THEIR ASS TO A NEIGH-boring fair to sell him. They had not gone far when they met with a troop of women collected around a well, talking and laughing. "Look there," cried one of them, "did you ever see such fellows, to be trudging along the road on foot when they might ride?" The Miller hearing this, quickly made his Son mount the Ass, and continued to walk along merrily by his side. Presently they came up to a group of old men in earnest debate. "There," said one

of them, "it proves what I was saying. What respect is shown to old age in these days? Do you see that idle lad riding while his old father has to walk? Get down, you young scapegrace, and let the old man rest his weary limbs." Upon this, the Miller made his Son dismount, and got up himself. In this manner they had not proceeded far when they met a company of women and children. "Why, you lazy old fellow," cried several tongues at once, "how can you ride upon the beast, while that poor little lad there can hardly keep pace by the side of you?" The good-natured Miller immediately took up his Son behind him. They had now almost reached the town. "Pray, honest friend," said a citizen, "is that Ass your own?" "Yes," replied the old man. "O, one would not have

thought so," said the other, "by the way you load him. Why, you two fellows are better able to carry the poor beast than he you." "Anything to please you," said the Miller; "we can but try." So, alighting with his Son, they tied the legs of the Ass together, and by the help of a pole endeavored to carry him on their shoulders over a bridge near the entrance of the town. This entertaining sight brought the people in crowds to laugh at it; till the Ass, not liking the noise, nor the strange handling that he was subject to, broke the cords that bound him, and, tumbling off the pole, fell into the river. Upon this, the old man, vexed and ashamed, made the best of his way home again, convinced that by trying to please everybody he had pleased nobody, and lost his Ass in the bargain.

He who tries to please everybody pleases nobody.

THE MULE

A MULE, WELL FED AND WORKED BUT LITTLE, FRISKED AND GAM-bolled about in the fields, and said to himself, "What strength, what spirits are mine! My father must surely have been a thoroughbred Horse." He soon after fell into the hands of another Master, and was worked hard and but scantily fed. Thoroughly jaded, he now said, "What could I have been thinking about the other day? I feel certain now that my father could only have been an Ass."

Depend not on ancestry.

THE TWO FOXES

Two Foxes once found their way into a hen-roost, where they killed the Cock, the Hens, and the Chickens, and began to feed upon them. One of the Foxes, who was young and inconsiderate, was for devouring them all upon the spot; the other, who was old and covetous, proposed to reserve some of them for another time. "For experience, child," said he, "has made me wise, and I have seen many unexpected events since I came into the world. Let us provide therefore, against what may happen, and not consume all our stores at one meal." "All this is wondrous wise," replied the young Fox, "but for my part I am resolved not to stir until I have eaten as much as will serve me a whole week; for who would be mad enough to return hither, where it is certain the owner of these fowls will watch for us, and if he catch us, will put us to death?" After this short discourse, each pursued his own scheme. The young Fox ate till he burst himself, and had scarcely strength enough to reach his hole before he died. The old one who thought it much better to deny his appetite for the present, and lay up provision for the future, returned the next day, and was killed by the farmer. Thus the young one came to grief through greed, and the old one through avarice.

Every age has its peculiar vice.

THE FOX AND THE GRAPES

A HUNGRY FOX ONE DAY CHANCED TO COME into a vineyard where he saw some fine ripe grapes hanging at a good height from the ground. He jumped at them, and made many other vain attempts to reach them. Finally, he walked off, grumbling to himself, "If those grapes had been good I would be disappointed. But they are green and sour."

It is easy to despise what you cannot get.

THE ASS AND THE GRASSHOPPERS

AN ASS, HAVING HEARD SOME GRASSHOPPERS CHIRPING, WAS highly enchanted; and, desiring to possess the same charms of melody, he demanded what sort of food they lived on to give them such beautiful voices. They replied, "The dew." The Ass resolved that he would live only upon dew, and in a short time died of hunger.

No two people can be treated alike.

THE HORSE AND THE STAG

THE HORSE HAVING QUARRELLED WITH THE STAG, AND BEING unable to revenge himself upon his enemy, came to a Man and begged his help. He allowed the Man to saddle and bridle him, and together they ran down the Stag and killed him. The Horse neighed with joy, and, thanking his rider warmly, asked him now to remove his saddle and let him go. "No, no," said the Man; "you are much too useful to me as you are." The Horse thenceforward served the Man, and found that he had gratified his need for revenge at the cost of his liberty.

Put bounds to your anger or it will put bounds to you.

THE RAVEN AND THE SERPENT

A HUNGRY RAVEN, SEARCHING FOR PREY, CAME across a Snake lying at full length on a sunny bank. He seized him in his horny beak and would have devoured him, but the Snake, twisting and turning about, bit the Raven with his venomous fangs, so that he died in great pain. "I am justly served," gasped the dying bird, "for trying to profit by injuring another."

Have regard for the rights of others.

THE LOBSTERS

It chanced on a time that the shell of a boiled Lobster was thrown on the seashore, where it was quickly espied by one of the same tribe, who, young, ignorant, and vain, viewed it with admiration and delight. "See," said she, addressing her mother, who was at her side; "behold the beauty of one of our family, thus decked out in noble scarlet, so rich in color that no coral can surpass it in brilliancy! I shall have no rest till I am equally as fine, and have ceased to see myself the dingy object I am at present." "Vain creature!" replied the mother; "know that this same tawdry finery which you so earnestly covet was only acquired by death. And learn from this terrible example to be humble and content, obscure, and safe."

Fine feathers are a sign neither of wealth nor of happiness.

THE WOLF AND THE MASTIFF

A WOLF WHO WAS ALMOST SKIN AND BONE—SO WELL DID THE Dogs of the neighborhood keep guard—met, one moonshiny night, a sleek Mastiff, who was, moreover, as strong as he was fat. The Wolf would gladly have supped off him, but saw there would first be a great fight, for which, in his condition, he was not prepared; so, bidding the Dog good night very humbly, he praised his good looks. "It would be easy for you," replied the Mastiff, "to get as fat as I am, if you liked. Quit this forest, where you and your fellows live so wretchedly, and often die with hunger. Follow me, and you shall fare much better." "What shall I have to do?" asked the Wolf. "Almost nothing," answered the Dog; "only chase away the beggars, and fawn upon the folks of the house. You will, in return, be paid with all sorts of nice things—bones of fowls and pigeons—to say nothing of many a friendly pat on the head." The Wolf, at the picture of so much comfort, nearly shed tears of joy. They trotted off together, but, as they went along, the Wolf noticed a bare spot on the Dog's neck. "What is that mark?" said he. "Oh, nothing," said the Dog. "How nothing?" urged the Wolf. "Just the merest trifle," answered the Dog; "the collar which I wear when I am tied up is the cause of it." "Tied up!" exclaimed the Wolf, with a sudden stop; "tied up! Can you not always, then, run where you please?" "Well, not quite always," said the Mastiff; "but what can that matter?" "It matters so much to me," rejoined the Wolf, "that your lot shall not be mine at any price"; and leaping away, he ran once more to his native forest.

Liberty is priceless.

THE FISHERMAN PIPING

A Fisherman skilled in music took his flute and his nets to the seashore. Standing on a projecting rock he played several tunes, in the hope that the fish, attracted by his melody, would, of their own accord, dance into his net, which he had placed below. At last, having long waited in vain, he laid aside his flute, and casting his net into the sea, made an excellent haul of fish. When he saw them leaping about in the net upon the rock he said: "O, you most perverse creatures, when I piped you would not dance, but now that I have ceased you do so merrily."

He achieves most who sticks to his trade.

THE HOUNDS IN COUPLES

A Huntsman was leading forth his Hounds one morning to the chase and had linked several of the young dogs in couples to prevent their following every scent and hunting disorderly, as their own inclinations and fancy should direct them. Among others, it was the fate of Jowler and Vixen to be thus yoked together. Jowler and Vixen were both young and inexperienced, but had for some time been constant companions, and seemed to have entertained a great fondness for each other; they used to be perpetually playing together, and in any quarrel that happened, always took one another's part; it might have been expected, therefore, that it would not be disagreeable to them to be still more closely united. However, it proved otherwise. They had not been long joined together before both parties began to express uneasiness at their present situation. Different inclinations and opposite wills began to discover and to exert themselves: if one chose to go this way, the other was as eager to take the contrary;

if one was pressing forward, the other was sure to lag behind; Vixen pulled back Jowler, and Jowler dragged along Vixen; Jowler growled at Vixen, and Vixen snapped at Jowler, till at last it came to a downright quarrel between them; and Jowler treated Vixen in a very rough and ungenerous manner, without any regard to the inferiority of her strength, or the tenderness of her sex. As they were thus continually vexing and tormenting one another, an old Hound, who had observed all that passed, came up to them, and thus reproved them: "What a couple of silly puppies you are, to be perpetually worrying yourselves at this rate! What hinders your going on peaceably and quietly together? Cannot you compromise the matter between you by each consulting the other's inclination a little? At least, try to make a virtue of necessity, and submit to what you cannot remedy; you cannot get rid of the chain, but you may make it fit easy upon you. I am an old dog; let my age and experience instruct you. When I was in the same circumstances with you, I soon found that thwarting my companion was only tormenting myself; and my yokefellow happily came into the same way of thinking. We endeavored to join in the same pursuits, and to follow one another's inclinations, and so we jogged on together, not only with ease and quiet, but with comfort and pleasure. We found, by experience, that mutual compliance not only compensates for liberty, but is even attended with a satisfaction and delight, beyond what liberty itself can give."

Mutual compliances are necessary to
matrimonial happiness.

THE HORSE AND THE HOG

A Hog that was lazily lying in the sun saw a Warhorse advancing, on his way to the battlefield. The Warhorse was gaily caparisoned, and proudly spurned the ground, as if impatient to charge the enemy. The Hog half lifted his head and, grunting, said to him, "What a fool you are to be so ready to rush to your death!" "Your speech," replied the Horse, "fits well a vile animal, that only lives to get fat and be killed by the knife. If I die on the field, I die where duty calls me, and I shall leave the memory of a good name behind."

'Tis not death but the manner of it which is important.

THE WOLF AND THE KID

A Wolf spied a Kid that had strayed to a distance from the herd, and pursued him. The Kid, finding that he could not escape, waited till the Wolf came up, and then assuming a cheerful tone, said, "I see clearly enough that I must be eaten, but I would fain die as pleasantly as I can. Give me, therefore, a few notes of the pipe you play so well, before I go to destruction." It seems that the Wolf was of a musical turn, and always carried his pipe with him. Flattered by the Kid's compliment, the Wolf played and the Kid danced, until the noise of the pipe brought the Dogs to the spot. The Wolf hastily fled, saying, "This is what comes when people will go meddling out of their profession. My business was to play the butcher, not the piper."

Stick to your task.

THE WILD AND THE TAME GEESE

Two Geese strayed from a farmyard, and swam down a stream to a large swamp, which afforded them an extensive range and plenty of food. A flock of Wild Geese frequently resorted to the same place; and though they were at first so shy as not to suffer the Tame ones to join them, by degrees they became well acquainted and associated freely together. One evening their cackling reached the ears of a Fox that was prowling at no great distance from the swamp. The artful plunderer directed his course through a wood on the borders of it, and was within a few yards of his prey before any of the Geese perceived him. But the alarm was given just as he was springing upon them, and the whole flock instantly ascended into the air, with loud and dissonant cries. "The Fox! The Fox!" the Wild Geese called as they rose swiftly out of his clutches; and they winged their flight into higher regions and were seen no more. "The Fox! The Fox!"

replied the two Tame Geese, rising after them; but being heavy, clumsy, and unused to using their wings, they soon dropped down, and became the victims of the Fox.

Those who aspire to a higher station should be able to maintain their position.

THE GRATEFUL EAGLE AND THE FOX

A MAN CAUGHT AN EAGLE IN A SNARE, CUT HIS WINGS CLOSE, and kept him chained to a stump in his yard. A kind-hearted Fowler, seeing the melancholy-looking bird, took pity on him, and bought him. He was now well treated, and his wings were allowed to grow. When they had grown again sufficiently for him to fly, the Fowler gave him his liberty. The first thing the bird caught was a fine fat Hare, which he brought and gratefully laid at the feet of his benefactor. A Fox, looking on, said that he would have done better to try to make friends with the first Man who had caught him, and who might, perhaps, catch him yet again, rather than with the second, from whom he had nothing to fear. "Your advice may do very well for a Fox," replied the Eagle; "but it is my nature to serve those who have been kind to me, rather than be governed by fear."

Fear commands poorer service than kindness.

THE BALD MAN AND THE FLY

A FLY SETTLED ON THE HEAD OF A BALD MAN AND BIT HIM. IN his eagerness to kill it, he hit himself a smart slap. But the Fly escaped, and said to him in derision, "You tried to kill me for just one little bite; what will you do to yourself now, for the heavy smack you have just given yourself?" "Oh, for that blow I bear no grudge," he replied, "for I never intended myself any harm; but as for you, you contemptible insect, who live by sucking human blood, I'd have borne a good deal more than that for the satisfaction of dashing the life out of you!"

No reprisal is too harsh for the contemptible.

THE ASS AND HIS MASTER

A DILIGENT ASS, DAILY LOADED BEYOND HIS STRENGTH BY A severe Master whom he had long served and who fed him very sparingly, happened one day in his old age to be laden with a more-than-ordinary burden of earthenware. His strength being much impaired, and the road deep and uneven, he unfortunately stumbled, and, unable to recover himself, fell down and broke all the vessels to pieces. His Master, transported with rage, began to beat him unmercifully, against which the poor Ass, lifting up his head as he lay on the ground, thus strongly remonstrated: "Unfeeling wretch! to thine own avaricious cruelty, in first pinching me of food, and then loading me beyond my strength, thou owest the misfortune for which I suffer!"

The cruel are quick to blame their victims for deserving ill-treatment.

THE COCK AND THE HORSES

A COCK ONCE GOT INTO A STABLE, AND WENT ABOUT NESTLING and scratching in the straw among the Horses, who every now and then would stamp and fling out their heels. So the Cock gravely set to work to admonish them. "Pray, my good friends, let us have a care," said he, "that we don't tread on one another."

Disinterested counsel is rare.

THE ASTRONOMER

AN ASTRONOMER USED TO GO OUT AT NIGHT TO OBSERVE THE stars. One evening, as he wandered through the suburbs with his whole attention fixed on the sky, he fell unawares into a ditch. While he lamented and bewailed his sores and bruises, and cried loudly for help, a neighbor ran to the ditch and learning what had happened said: "Hark ye, old fellow, why, in striving to pry into what is in Heaven, do you not manage to see what is on Earth?"

Do not overlook the ordinary for the wondrous.

JUPITER'S TWO WALLETS

WHEN JUPITER MADE MAN, HE GAVE HIM TWO WALLETS—ONE for his neighbor's faults, the other for his own. He threw them over the Man's shoulder, so that one hung in front and the other behind. The Man kept the one in front for his neighbor's faults, and the one behind for his own; so that while the first was always under his nose, it took some pains to see the latter. This custom, which began thus early, is not quite unknown at the present day.

One can always see his neighbor's faults more easily
than his own.

THE EAGLE AND THE OWL

THE EAGLE AND THE OWL, AFTER MANY QUARRELS, SWORE THAT they would be friends forever, and that they would never harm each other's young ones. "But do you know my little ones?" said the Owl. "If you do not, I fear it will go hard with them when you find them." "No, I have never seen them," replied the Eagle. "The greater your loss," said the Owl; "they are the sweetest, prettiest things in the world. Such dear eyes! such charming plumage! such winning little ways! You'll know them, now, from my description." A short time after, the Eagle found the little Owls in a hollow tree. "These hideous, staring frights, at any rate, cannot be neighbor Owl's fine brood," said he; "so I may make away with them without the least misgiving." So saying he made a meal of them. The Owl, finding her young ones gone, loaded the Eagle with reproaches. "Nay," answered the Eagle, "blame yourself rather than me. If you paint with such flattering colors, it is not my fault if I do not recognize your portraits."

Love should not blind truth.

THE CROW AND THE PITCHER

A Crow, ready to die with thirst, flew with joy to a pitcher, hoping to find some water in it. He found some there, to be sure, but only a little drop at the bottom, which he was quite unable to reach. He then tried to overturn the Pitcher, but it was

too heavy. So he gathered up some pebbles, with which the ground was covered, and, taking them one by one in his beak, dropped them into the Pitcher. By this means the water gradually reached the top, and he was able to drink at his ease.

Necessity is the mother
of invention.

THE PEASANT AND THE APPLE TREE

A Peasant had in his garden an apple tree, which bore no fruit, but only served as a harbor for the sparrows and grasshoppers. He resolved to cut it down and, taking his axe in his hand, made a bold stroke at its roots. The grasshoppers and sparrows entreated him not to cut down the tree that sheltered them, but to spare it, and they would sing to him and lighten his labors. He paid no attention to their request, but gave the tree a second and a third blow with his axe; when he reached the hollow of the tree, he found a hive full of honey. Greatly delighted, he threw down his axe, and thereafter took great care of the tree.

Self-interest alone moves some men.

THE MAN, THE HORSE, THE OX, AND THE DOG

ONE WINTER'S DAY, DURING A SEVERE STORM, A HORSE, AN OX, and a Dog came and begged for shelter in the house of a Man. He readily admitted them, and, as they were cold and wet, he lit a fire for their comfort: and he put oats before the Horse, and hay before the Ox, while he fed the Dog with the remains of his own dinner. When the storm abated, and they were about to depart, they determined to show their gratitude in the following way. They divided the life of Man among them, and each endowed one part of it with the qualities which were peculiarly his own. The Horse took youth, and hence young men are high-mettled and impatient of restraint; the Ox took middle age, and accordingly men in middle life are steady and hard-working; while the Dog took old age, which is the reason why old men are so often peevish and ill-tempered, and, like dogs, attached chiefly to those who look to their comfort, while they are disposed to snap at those who are unfamiliar or distasteful to them.

Life, like Nature, has different seasons,
each with its own character.

THE LION, THE BEAR,
THE MONKEY, AND THE FOX

THE TYRANT OF THE FOREST ISSUED A PROCLAMATION, COM-
manding all his subjects to repair immediately to his royal den.
Among the rest, the Bear made his appearance; but pretending to
be offended with the steams that issued from the monarch's apartments, he was imprudent enough to hold his nose in his majesty's
presence. This insolence was so highly resented that the Lion, in
a rage, laid him dead at his feet. The Monkey, observing what
had passed, trembled for his carcass, and attempted to concili-
ate favor by the most abject flattery. He began with protesting,
that for his part, he thought the apartments were perfumed with
Arabian spices, and exclaiming against the rudeness of the Bear,
admired the beauty of his majesty's paws, so happily formed, he
said, to correct the insolence of clowns. This fulsome adulation,
instead of being received as he expected, proved no less offensive
than the rudeness of the Bear, and the courtly Monkey was in like
manner extended by the side of Sir Bruin. And now his majesty
cast his eye upon the Fox. "Well, Fox," said he, "and what scent
do you discover here?" "Great Prince," replied the cautious Fox,
"my nose was never esteemed my most distinguishing sense, and
at present I would by no means venture to give my opinion, as I
have unfortunately got a terrible cold."

*It is often more prudent to suppress
our sentiments than either to flatter, or to rail.*

THE MASTIFF AND THE CURS

A STOUT AND HONEST MASTIFF THAT GUARDED THE VILLAGE where he lived against robbers was one day walking with one of his Puppies by his side when all the little Dogs in the street gathered about him and barked at him. The Puppy was so enraged at this insult that he asked his father why he did not fall upon them and tear them to pieces. To which the Mastiff answered, with great composure of mind, "If there were no Curs, I should be no Mastiff."

Nobility is its own defense.

THE LAMB AND THE WOLF

A FLOCK OF SHEEP WERE FEEDING IN A MEADOW WHILE THEIR Dogs were asleep and their Shepherd at a distance, playing on his pipe beneath the shade of a spreading elm. A young, inexperienced Lamb, observing a half-starved Wolf peering through the pales of the enclosure, entered into conversation with him. "Pray, what are you seeking for here?" said the Lamb. "I am looking," replied the Wolf, "for some tender grass; for nothing, you know, is more pleasant than to feed in a fresh pasture, and to slake one's thirst at a crystal stream, both of which I perceive you enjoy here. Happy creature," continued he, "how much I envy your lot, who are in full possession of the utmost I desire; for philosophy has long taught me to be satisfied with a little!" "It seems, then," returned the Lamb, "that those who say you feed on flesh accuse you falsely, since a little grass will easily content you. If this be true, let us for the future live like brethren, and feed together." So saying, the simple Lamb crept through the fence, and at once became a prey to the pretended philosopher, and a sacrifice to his own inexperience and credulity.

Experience is a dear school, but fools will learn in no other.

THE BEAR AND THE FOX

THE BEAR IS SAID TO BE UNWILLING TO TOUCH THE DEAD BODY of a Man; and one of the animals was once heard making a virtue of this peculiarity. "Such is my regard for mankind," said he, "that nothing on earth would induce me to injure a human corpse." "Your kindness would impress me much more," said a Fox who was listening to this speech, "if I could believe that you paid the same respect to the living that you profess to do to the dead."

Regard is not shown in half-service.

THE DEBTOR AND HIS SOW

A MAN OF ATHENS FELL INTO DEBT AND WAS PRESSED FOR THE money by his Creditor; but he had no means of paying at the time, so he begged for delay. But the creditor refused and said he must pay at once. Then the Debtor fetched a Sow—the only one he had—and took her to market to offer her for sale. It happened that his Creditor was there too. Presently a Buyer came along and asked if the Sow produced good litters. "Yes," said the Debtor, "very fine ones; and the remarkable thing is that she produces females at the Mysteries and males at the Panathenea." (Festivals these were: and the Athenians always sacrifice a Sow at one, and a Boar at the other; while at the Dionysia they sacrifice a kid.) At that the Creditor, who was standing by, put in, "Don't be surprised, sir; why, still better, at the Dionysia this Sow has kids!"

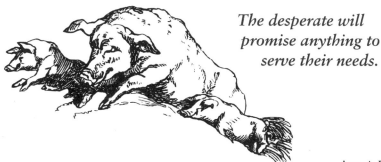

The desperate will promise anything to serve their needs.

THE CONCEITED OWL

A YOUNG OWL, HAVING ACCIDENTALLY SEEN HIMSELF IN A CRYStal fountain, conceived the highest opinion of his personal perfections. "It is time," said he, "that Hymen should give me children as beautiful as myself, to be the glory of the night, and the ornament of our groves. What pity would it be if the race of the most accomplished of birds should be extinct for my want of a mate! Happy the female who is destined to spend her life with me!" Full of these self-approving thoughts, he entreated the Crow to propose a match between him and the royal daughter of the Eagle. "Do you imagine," said the Crow, "that the noble Eagle, whose pride it is to gaze on the brightest of the heavenly luminaries, will consent to marry his daughter to you, who cannot so much as open your eyes whilst it is daylight?" But the conceited Owl was deaf to all that his friend could urge; who, after much persuasion, was at length prevailed upon to undertake the commission. His proposal was received in the manner that might be expected: the King of Birds laughed him to scorn. However, being a monarch of some humor, he ordered him to acquaint the Owl that if he would meet him the next morning at sunrise in the middle of the sky, he would consent to give him his daughter in marriage. The presumptuous Owl undertook to perform that condition; but being dazzled with the sun, and his head growing giddy, he fell from his height upon a rock; from whence being pursued by a flight of birds, he was glad at last to make his escape into the hollow of an old oak, where he passed the remainder of his days in that obscurity for which nature designed him.

Schemes of ambition, without proper talent,
always end in disgrace. AESOP'S FABLES

THE CAT AND THE BIRDS

A Cat, hearing that the Birds in a certain cage were ailing, dressed himself up as a physician and, taking with him his cane and the instruments becoming his profession, went to the cage, knocked at the door, and inquired of the inmates how they all did, saying that if they were ill, he would be happy to prescribe for them and cure them. They replied, "We are all very well, and shall continue so, if you will only be good enough to go away and leave us as we are."

Some cures are worse than the disease.

THE TWO RATS

A CUNNING OLD RAT DISCOVERED IN HIS ROUNDS A MOST tempting piece of cheese, which was placed in a trap. But being well aware that if he touched it he would be caught, he slyly sought one of his young friends, and, under the mask of friendship, informed him of the prize. "I cannot use it myself," said he, "for I have just made a hearty meal." The inexperienced youngster thanked him with gratitude for the news, and heedlessly sprang upon the tempting bait; on which the trap closed and instantly destroyed him. His companion, being now quite secure, quietly ate up the cheese.

Do not listen to every passerby.

THE LION AND THE SNAKE

A LOUDLY LION, WHO WAS SEEKING FOR HIS PREY, BY CHANCE saw a Snake basking in the sun, when, being rather sharp-set by hunger, and disappointed in his object, he, with a haughty air, spurned the reptile with his paw, as not being agreeable to his stomach. But the enraged Snake turned on him, gave him a mortal sting, and said: "Die, imperious tyrant! and let thy example show that no power can always save a despot, and that even reptiles have rights."

The tyrant lays himself open to attack.

THE OSTRICH AND THE PELICAN

THE OSTRICH ONE DAY MET THE PELICAN AND OBSERVED HER breast all bloody. "Good God!" he said to her, "what is the matter? What accident has befallen you? You certainly have been seized by some savage beast of prey, and have with difficulty escaped from his merciless claws." "Do not be surprised, friend," replied the Pelican; "no such accident, nor indeed anything more than common, hath happened to me. I have only been engaged in my ordinary employment of tending my nest, of feeding my dear little ones, and nourishing them with the vital blood from my bosom." "Your answer," returned the Ostrich, "astonishes me still more than the horrid figure you make. What, is this your practice, to tear your own flesh, to spill your own blood, and to sacrifice yourself in this cruel manner to the importunate cravings of your young ones? I know not which to pity most, your misery or your folly. Be advised by me: have some regard for yourself, and leave off this barbarous custom of mangling your own body; as for your children, commit them to the care of Providence, and make yourself quite easy about them. My example may be of use to you. I lay my eggs upon the ground, and just cover them lightly over with sand; if they have the good luck to escape being crushed by the tread of man or beast, the warmth of the sun broods upon, and hatches them, and in due time my young ones come forth; I leave them to be nursed by nature, and fostered by the elements; I give myself no trouble about them, and I neither know nor care what becomes of them." "Unhappy wretch," said the Pelican, "who hardenest thyself against thy own offspring, and through want of natural affection renderest thy travail fruitless to thyself! Who knowest not the sweets of a parent's anxiety; the tender delights of a mother's sufferings! It is not I, but thou, that art cruel to thy own flesh. Thy insensibility may exempt thee from a temporary inconvenience, and an inconsiderable pain, but at the same time it makes thee inattentive to a most necessary duty, and incapable of relishing the pleasure that attends it; a pleasure, the most exquisite that nature hath indulged to us; in which pain itself is swallowed up and lost, or only serves to heighten the enjoyment."

The pleasures of parental fondness make large amends
for all its anxieties.

THE SPANIEL AND THE MASTIFF

A GOOD-NATURED SPANIEL overtook a surly MASTIFF as he was traveling upon the high road. The Spaniel, although a complete stranger to the Mastiff, very civilly accosted him; and if it would be no intrusion, he said, he should be glad to bear him company on his way. The Mastiff, who happened not to be altogether in so growling a mood as usual, accepted the proposal, and they very amicably pursued their journey together. In the midst of their conversation they arrived at the next village, where the Mastiff began to display his ugly temper by an unprovoked attack upon every Dog he met. The villagers immediately sallied forth with great indignation to rescue their pets; and falling upon our two friends without distinction or mercy, most cruelly treated the poor Spaniel for no other reason but his being found in bad company.

Much of every man's good or ill fortune depends upon his choice of friends.

THE PEACOCK

THE PEACOCK, WHO AT FIRST WAS DISTINGUISHED ONLY BY A crest of feathers, proferred a petition to Juno that he might be honored also with a train. As the bird was a particular favorite, Juno readily enough assented; and his train was ordered to surpass that of every fowl in the creation. The Peacock, conscious of his superb appearance, thought it requisite to assume a proportionable dignity of gait and manners. The common poultry of the farmyard were quite astonished at his magnificence; and even the Pheasants themselves beheld him with an eye of envy. But when he attempted to fly, he perceived himself to have sacrificed all his activity to ostentation; and that he was encumbered by the pomp in which he placed his glory.

The parade and ceremony belonging to the great are often a restraint upon their freedom and dignity.

THE FARMER AND HIS DOG

A FARMER WHO HAD GONE INTO HIS FIELD TO MEND A GAP IN one of his fences found, at his return, the cradle in which he had left his only child asleep turned upside down, the clothes all torn and bloody, and his Dog lying near it, besmeared also with blood. Thinking that the animal had destroyed his child, he instantly dashed out his brains with the hatchet in his hand. When turning up the cradle, he found his child unhurt, and an enormous Serpent lying dead on the floor, killed by that faithful Dog, he lamented that the beast's courage and fidelity in preserving the life of his son deserved another kind of reward.

It is dangerous to give way to the blind impulse of a sudden passion.

THE MONKEY AND THE CAMEL

THE BEASTS OF THE FOREST GAVE A SPLENDID ENTERTAINMENT at which the Monkey stood up and danced. Having vastly delighted the assembly, he sat down amid universal applause. The Camel, envious of the praises bestowed on the Monkey, and desirous to divert to himself the favor of the guests, proposed to stand up in his turn, and dance for their amusement. He moved about in so utterly ridiculous a manner, that the beasts, in a fit of indignation, set upon him with clubs and drove him out of the assembly.

It is absurd to ape our betters.

THE MICE AND THE TRAP

ONCE UPON A TIME SOME MICE SAW A BIT OF TOASTED BACON
hanging up in a very little room, the door of which, being open,
enticed them to fall to work on the dainty morsel with greedy
appetites. But two or three of them took particular notice that
there was but one way into the room, and, therefore, but one way
to get out of it; so that if the door by misfortune or art should
chance to be shut, they would all inevitably be taken. They could
not, therefore, bring themselves to enter, but said that they would
rather content themselves with homely fare in plenty, than for the
sake of a dainty bit run the risk of being taken and lost forever.
The other Mice, however, declared that they saw no danger, and
ran into the room and began to eat the bacon with great delight.
But they soon heard the door fall down, and saw that they were
all taken. Then the fear of approaching death so seized them that

they found no relish for the delicious food, but stood shivering and fasting until the Cook who had set the Trap came and put an end to them. The wise Mice, who had contented themselves with their usual food, fled into their holes, and by that means preserved their lives.

He who embarks upon an enterprise should be able to see his way out of it.

THE HARE AFRAID OF HIS EARS

THE LION, BEING ONCE BADLY HURT BY THE HORNS OF A GOAT, went into a great rage, and swore that every animal with horns should be banished from his kingdom. Goats, Bulls, Rams, Deer, and every living thing with horns had quickly to be off on pain of death. A Hare, seeing from his shadow how long his ears were, was in great fear lest they should be taken for horns. "Goodbye, my friend," said he to a Cricket who, for many a long summer evening, had chirped to him where he lay dozing: "I must be off from here. My ears are too much like horns to allow me to be comfortable." "Horns!" exclaimed the Cricket, "do you take me for a fool? You no more have horns than I have." "Say what you please," replied the Hare, "were my ears only half as long as they are, they would be quite long enough for any one to lay hold of who wished to make them out to be horns."

Avoid the appearance of evil.

THE NURSE AND THE WOLF

As a Wolf was hunting up and down for his supper, he passed by the door of a house where a little child was crying loudly. "Hold your tongue," said the Nurse to the child, "or I'll throw you to the Wolf." The Wolf, hearing this, waited near the house, expecting that she would keep her word. The Nurse, however, when the child was quiet, changed her tone, and said, "If the naughty Wolf comes now, we'll beat his brains out for him." The Wolf thought it was then high time to be off. "Serves me right," growled he; "I shall starve to death if I listen to idle threats."

He who threatens most does least.

THE THREE TRADESMEN

The citizens of a certain city were debating about the best material to use in the fortifications which were about to be erected for the greater security of the town. A Carpenter got up and advised the use of wood, which he said was readily procurable and easily worked. A Stonemason objected to wood on the ground that it was so inflammable, and recommended stones instead. Then a Tanner got on his legs and said, "In my opinion there's nothing like leather."

Every man for himself.

THE MOCKINGBIRD

There is a certain bird in America which has the faculty of mimicking the notes of every other songster, without being able himself to add any original strains to the concert. One of these Mockingbirds displayed his talent of ridicule among the branches of a venerable wood. " 'Tis very well," said a little warbler, speaking for all the rest; "we grant you that our music is not without its faults; but why will you not favor us with a strain of your own?"

Many ridicule the things that they themselves cannot do.

THE ANT AND THE COCOON

An Ant, nimbly running about in the sunshine in search of food, came across a Cocoon that was very near its time of change. The Cocoon moved its tail, and thus attracted the attention of the Ant, who then saw for the first time that it was alive. "Poor creature!" cried the Ant disdainfully; "what a sad fate is yours! While I can run hither and thither, at my pleasure, and, if I wish, ascend the tallest tree, you lie imprisoned here in your shell, with power only to move a joint or two of your scaly tail." The Cocoon heard all this, but did not try to make any reply. A few days after, when the Ant passed that way again, nothing but the shell remained. Wondering what had become of its contents, he felt himself suddenly shaded and fanned by the gorgeous wings of a beautiful Butterfly. "Behold in me," said the Butterfly, "your much-pitied friend! Boast now of your powers to run and climb as long as you can get me to listen." So saying, the Butterfly rose in the air, and, borne along on the summer breeze, was soon lost to the sight of the Ant forever.

Judge not alone by the present.

THE OX AND THE FROG

An Ox grazing in a meadow chanced to set his foot on a young Frog and crushed him to death. His brothers and sisters, who were playing near, at once ran to tell their mother what had happened. "The monster that did it, mother, was such a size!" said they. The mother, who was a vain old thing, thought that she could easily make herself as large. "Was it as big as this?" she asked, blowing and puffing herself out. "Oh, much bigger than that!" replied the young Frogs. "As this, then?" cried she, puffing and blowing again with all her might. "Nay, mother," said they; "if you were to try till you burst yourself, you would never be so big." The silly old Frog tried to puff herself out still more, and burst herself indeed.

People are ruined by attempting a greatness
to which they have no claim.

THE FOX AND THE CAT

A Fox and a Cat, traveling together, sought to relieve the tediousness of their journey by moralizing. "Of all the moral virtues," exclaimed the Fox, "mercy is surely the noblest! What say you, my sage friend, is it not so?" "Undoubtedly," replied the Cat, with a most demure countenance; "nothing is more becoming in a creature of any sensibility than compassion." While they were thus complimenting each other on the wisdom of their views, a Wolf darted out from a wood upon a flock of Sheep which were feeding in an adjacent meadow, and without being in the least affected by the piteous cries of a poor Lamb, devoured it before their eyes. "Horrible cruelty!" exclaimed the Cat. "Why does he not feed on vermin, instead of making his barbarous meals on such innocent creatures?" The Fox agreed with his friend in the observation, to which he added some very pathetic remarks on the odiousness of such conduct. Their indignation was rising in its warmth and zeal when they arrived at a little cottage by the wayside, where the tenderhearted Fox immediately cast his eye upon a fine Cock that was strutting about in the yard. And now, adieu moralizing, he leaped over the pales, and without any sort of scruple, demolished his prize in an instant. In the meanwhile, a plump Mouse, which ran out of the stable, totally put to flight our Cat's philosophy, who fell to the repast without the least commiseration.

*It is a common habit to talk of what is right
and good, and to do what is quite the reverse.*

THE GEESE AND THE CRANES

A FLOCK OF GEESE AND A COVEY OF CRANES USED TO FEED together in a wheat field, where the grain was just ripening for harvest. One day the owner of the field came up and surprised them. The Cranes were thin and light, and easily flew away. But the Geese were heavy and fat, and many of them were caught.

Many criminals go unpunished.

THE FOX AND THE TIGER

A SKILLFUL ARCHER, COMING INTO THE WOODS, DIRECTED HIS arrows so well that the beasts fled in dismay. The Tiger, however, told them not to be afraid, for he would singly engage their enemy, and drive him from their domain. He had scarcely spoken, when an arrow pierced his ribs and lodged in his side. The Fox asked him, slyly, what he thought of his opponent now. "Ah!" replied the Tiger, writhing with pain, "I find that I was mistaken in my reckoning."

Knowledge is power.

THE TRAVELERS AND THE CROW

SOME TRAVELERS SETTING OUT ON A JOURNEY HAD NOT PRO-ceeded far when a one-eyed Crow flew across their path. This they took for a bad omen, and it was proposed that they should give up their plan for that day, at least, and turn back again. "What nonsense!" said one of the Travelers, who was of a mocking and merry disposition. "If this Crow could foresee what is to happen to us, he would be equally knowing on his own account; and in that case, do you think he would have been silly enough to go where his eye was to be knocked out of his head?"

Common sense is better than auguries.

Index to the Fables

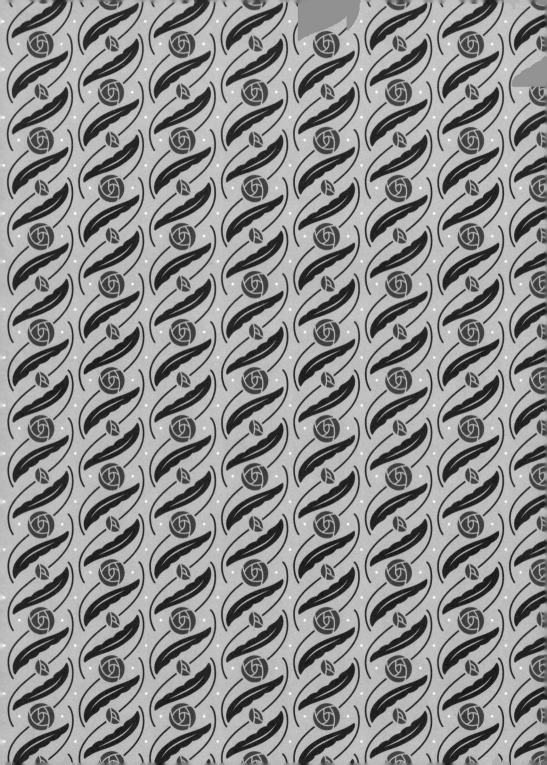